HANDBOOK FOR WILLIAM

"I send you this little book written down in my name, that you may read it for your education, as a kind of mirror," wrote a Frankish noblewoman named Dhuoda to her young son William in the middle of the ninth century. Intended as a guide to right conduct, the book was to be shared in time with William's younger brother. Dhuoda's situation was poignant. Her husband, Bernard, the count of Septimania, was generally away and she was separated from her children—William was being held at the court of Charlemagne's grandson Charles the Bald as a guarantee of his father's loyalty, and the younger son's whereabouts was unknown. As war raged in the crumbling Carolingian Empire, the grieving mother, fearing for the spiritual and physical welfare of her absent sons, began in 841 to write her loving counsel in a handbook. Two years later she sent it to William.

One of the few surviving texts written by a woman of the Middle Ages, Dhuoda's *Liber manualis* was available in only two faulty Latin manuscripts until a third, superior one was discovered in the 1950s. This English translation by Carol Neel, based on the 1975 critical edition and French translation by Pierre Riché, will bring the work to a wider audience. *Handbook for William* memorably expresses Dhuoda's maternal feelings, religious fervor, and learning. In teaching her children how they might flourish in God's eyes, as well as humanity's, Dhuoda reveals the authority of Carolingian women in aristocratic households. She dwells on family relations, social order, the connection between religious and military responsibility, and, always, the central place of Christian devotion in a noble life.

Carol Neel, whose publications include articles in scholarly journals, is an associate professor of history at Colorado College. In her introduction she discusses the sociopolitical, literary, and theological background of *Handbook for William*.

HANDBOOK FOR

William

A Carolingian Woman's Counsel for Her Son

by Dhuoda

Translated and with an introduction by Carol Neel

University of Nebraska Press: Lincoln and London

Based on the French edition
published as
Manuel pour mon fils, edited by
Pierre Riché,
copyright © Les Éditions
du cerf, 1975
The paper in this book meets the
minimum requirements
of American National Standard for
Information Sciences –
Permanence of Paper for Printed
Library Materials, ANSI Z39.48-1984.

Library of Congress
Cataloging in Publication Data
Dhuoda.
[Liber manualis. English]
Handbook for William : a Carolingian woman's counsel for
her son / by Dhuoda : translated
and edited by Carol Neel.
p. cm. – (Regents studies in
medieval culture)
Translation of: Liber manualis.
Includes bibliographical
references. ISBN 0-8032-1685-8
(alkaline paper)
1. Teenage boys – Conduct of life –
Handbooks, manuals, etc. –
Early works to 1800. 2. Teenage
boys – Religious life –
Handbooks, manuals, etc. – Early
works to 1800.
3. Christian life – Middle Ages,
600-1500 – Handbooks,
manuals, etc. I. Neel, Carol.
II. Title. III. Series.
BJ1600.D4813 1991 170'.835'1-dc20
90-43359 CIP

BJ
1600
.D4813
1991

Contents

ACKNOWLEDGMENTS

This translation project was supported by the Colorado College and the Newberry Library.

Thanks are due here to those individuals who contributed to the completion of the English text and commentary: Pierre Riché of the University of Paris, the editors of Sources Chrétiennes, and Editions du Cerf for their permission to use Professor Riché's edition as the translation's basis;[1] Glenn Olsen of the University of Utah and James O'Donnell of the University of Pennsylvania, along with the readers of the University of Nebraska Press, for their valuable suggestions on the text and Introduction; Barbara Neilon and Diane Burgner of the Colorado College Library for their able bibliographical assistance; and the many Colorado College students who have, in the past several years, responded to Dhuoda's work and my commentary with valuable questions.

Others have contributed to this translation's completion in less specific but no less important ways: Glenn Brooks, in whose deanship at the Colorado College this and many like projects found enthusiastic support; James Trissel, whose patience with this translation has outlasted the time its completion required; and Margaret and Clare Trissel, who have provided the consistent reminder that, despite its separation in time and space, Dhuoda's world was not fundamentally different from the translator's own.

Introduction

Dhuoda and Her Handbook

Dhuoda, a Frankish noblewoman, wrote *Handbook for William* in the middle of the ninth century. In its original Latin, Dhuoda's text is conventionally called *Liber manualis*, "handbook," without specific mention of its intended audience. The author nevertheless seems to have wished that it be more specifically identified. The present translation reflects her emphasis in the *Handbook*'s opening and closing lines that she wrote it for the use of her elder son, from whom she was separated when he was fourteen years old. The author here enjoins the adolescent William to use his *Handbook* carefully for his own benefit. She urges too that he employ it in the instruction of his infant brother when the younger child is old enough to understand (1.7; 10.1; 10.4).[1] Dhuoda's *Handbook for William*, then, presents itself as a source of consolation for a grieving mother. Through this work, she represents her influence on and her love for her absent children.

Dhuoda began the *Handbook* in 841 and sent it to William in 843, during an extended period of warfare among the Frankish nobility. The emperor Louis the Pious, Charlemagne's son, had died in 840. His three sons Lothar, Louis the German, and Charles the Bald then battled each other over the partition of their father's vast territories, eventually dividing Europe among themselves in the Treaty of Verdun. According to this agreement, struck in the same year Dhuoda set aside her work, Louis maintained his authority over the eastern Franks, Charles established his power in the west, and their overlord, Lothar, held a wide strip of territory cutting Europe north to south from the Low Countries to Italy. But this uneasy resolution, portentous for the subsequent development of European nations, was unforeseen by the *Handbook*'s author.

As Dhuoda wrote, enmity within the Carolingian house had worsened steadily since Louis the Pious's sons had first begun, over ten years previously, to rebel against their father's authority. This strife still seemed far from settlement. Meanwhile the nobility, which since Charlemagne's time had increasingly come to define its power in terms of its administration of a European empire, was embroiled in the Carolingian heirs' struggle for power.[2] The same events that led to the empire's division at Verdun kept Dhuoda from her sons and occasioned the composition of *Handbook for William*.

Although Dhuoda's husband, Bernard, count of Septimania, was one of the most prominent Frankish magnates of the generation after Charlemagne,[3] the *Handbook* author herself is not mentioned in any ninth-century work except her own. A few details of her life are recorded in her text. Dhuoda writes that she was married in the 820s at the Carolingian capital, Aachen. Evidently both she and her husband were members of powerful families,[4] but neither Dhuoda's high rank nor her marriage to a great lord brought her comfort or security. She seems to have seen little of Bernard for the fourteen years between the birth of William in 826 and the birth of their second son in 841 (prol. ["Preface"]).[5] During that period, according to her account, she struggled to maintain her husband's authority on the tense southern border of Francia. In isolation and in hardship, Dhuoda preserved Frankish Septimania, fulfilling its absent count's administrative and military responsibilities on Louis the Pious's behalf (10.4).[6]

Other ninth-century records reveal that throughout Bernard's marriage to Dhuoda, the count of Septimania traveled Europe from the Danube to the Loire as the virtual vice-emperor. From 831, when Louis appointed Bernard his chamberlain and defender against his rebellious sons, Dhuoda's husband's preeminence and power attracted the enmity and accusations of other Frankish magnates.[7] In 841 after the emperor's death, Bernard—like many other powerful nobles—scrambled to secure his own authority as the Carolingian heirs fought over the old emperor's lands. By the time Dhuoda undertook the composition of her handbook from her isolated residence at Uzès in the

Rhone Valley (prol. ["Preface"]), her husband had been forced to accept the authority of Louis's youngest son, Charles the Bald, whose kingship among the western Franks Bernard seems initially to have opposed and who now accepted the loyalty of his father's dangerously powerful friend only with guarantees.[8]

Among those pledges was Bernard and Dhuoda's son William, who at the time of his mother's writing has been taken away into the company of the same king, himself still only a very young man. Their second child, Dhuoda's infant, has been removed as well, although the mother is not sure where. William seems to have been a hostage against his father's betrayal of Charles;[9] the baby has disappeared with his father and the bishop of Uzès, probably because Bernard wished to keep one of his heirs secure in his immediate presence (prol. ["Preface"]). Dhuoda, isolated in her refuge near Avignon, fears for her children's lives and is convinced that her own death is imminent. Her tone is urgent. From time to time her apprehension and grief break the pattern of her exposition (10.4), yet she remains optimistic that the future holds better for William and his little brother.

The text translated here stands as a memorial to the failure of Dhuoda's hopes. Within the next few years her husband was executed by Charles the Bald, and her son William was killed in an attempt to avenge his father. Dhuoda's second child, whose career is difficult to trace in the general confusion in southern Francia during his lifetime, probably was Bernard Plantevelue—Hairyfeet—who attempted to murder Charles in 856. If he was Hairyfeet, Dhuoda's younger son survived to enjoy the king's pardon, to found the medieval duchy of Aquitaine, and to father William the Pious, who endowed the preeminent medieval Benedictine abbey, Cluny.[10] As for Dhuoda herself, she may have predeceased her husband and her elder son, for her *Handbook* repeatedly describes her ill health (10.1; 10.2; 10.4). She may never have realized how little help her written advice brought William, at least in his secular life.

Dhuoda nevertheless sought in *Handbook for William* to teach her children how they might flourish in God's eyes as well as men's. The contribution of her descendant William the Pious to European monastic revival was in keeping with his grandmother's wishes for her descendants, even though there is no reason to believe he knew her text.

Dhuoda, along with famous members of her husband's lineage before and after their generation, saw Christian devotion as central to their life among the nobility; in this she and her male relations were characteristic of the Carolingian Franks. The family into which Dhuoda married, about which we know a great deal more than we do about her own ancestry,[11] was typical of the ninth-century nobility in committing its resources to the establishment of religious life even as it fought within itself and against the pagan invaders of Charlemagne's immense territorial legacy. William of Gellone, the father of Dhuoda's warlord husband, Bernard, founded one of the great abbeys of southern Francia and ended his life there as a monk.[12] As J. M. Wallace-Hadrill noted in his standard survey of early Middle Ages, Bernard of Septimania and his lineage—"cutting throats, but endowing churches"— were the epitome of Frankish aristocratic values.[13] Dhuoda's counsel for her children must be seen in the context of such men, and of the unremitting violence of the ninth century.

The Importance of Dhuoda's Text

Handbook for William is a lonely text because its intended influence was truncated by its addressee's death. But it is lonely as well in that the work, a substantial text written by a woman, is the only such book to have survived from the Carolingian period.[14] In the course of Dhuoda's instruction on how William may best grow up to assume his place among the Frankish magnates, the author addresses such topics as family relations, social order, and the connection between religious and military responsibility. Her handbook throws welcome light on women's history, the history of childhood, and the self-perception of the Frankish nobility. The Carolingian Renaissance, as the cultural revival ensuing from Charlemagne's reign is often called, left many literary remains that testify to the liveliness of its intellectual life, but the overwhelming majority of ninth-century books are the works of male clerics. Dhuoda's work, a married woman's book, makes at least a partial break with that monopoly, to the benefit of our investigation of a ninth-century world whose many laypeople, women, and children left relatively few traces in the records of its churchmen.

Dhuoda's handbook has nevertheless been surprisingly little studied. Until 1975 it was available only in a nineteenth-century publication based on two faulty manuscripts.[15] A third medieval copy, in many instances a better witness to the text than either other extant manuscript, was identified by André Vernet in the 1950s.[16] Subsequently Pierre Riché, whose later magisterial work on Carolingian education is rooted in a study of Dhuoda's handbook, undertook a critical edition and French translation. After some delay, and with Bernard de Vrégille and Claude Mondésert completing the translation, Riché published Dhuoda's text in 1975.[17] His edition set aside many of the textual problems that had previously limited the usefulness—and had even cast doubt on the authenticity—of Dhuoda's work.[18]

Riché established that Dhuoda's intellectual background was representative of the lay education supported by Charlemagne and continued in the time of her own upbringing, in the reign of Louis the Pious.[19] He further confirmed that this author was, like her husband, Bernard of Septimania, a member of the Frankish nobility that was relocated across Europe, in their case to the old Visigothic territory in southernmost Francia, to administer Carolingian domains.[20] In this regard as well, Dhuoda's experience was typical of that of contemporary nobles. Riché thus clarified the cultural and biographical contexts of Dhuoda's text, as well as demonstrated the uniqueness of her handbook as the work of a lay noblewoman of the central ninth century.

Since the appearance of Riché's edition, Dhuoda's handbook has received considerable scholarly attention. It has been read, in general accordance with its editor's interpretation, as evidence of a strongly patriarchal organization among noble families in the central ninth century and of the weakness of Carolingian women in controlling their own and their families' lives. Peter Dronke, for instance, viewing Dhuoda among medieval women writers and focusing on her handbook's literary aspects, has focused on the tentativeness of her self-assertion as author and on her lament for her personal circumstances.[21] Constance Bouchard has found, in Dhuoda's aggrandizement of the importance of her husband's lineage, confirmation that patrilineal kinship ties—the father's ancestry—overshadowed matrilineal connections in Carolingian nobles' understanding of family relations.[22] Yet more recently, Rosamond McKitterick has seen Dhuoda's evident learning as characteristic of the heretofore underestimated literacy of the Frankish lay nobility, especially women.[23]

Clearly, *Handbook for William* is of interest to many readers for whom its Latin text is inaccessible but for whom it may clarify many issues in the intellectual lives and social roles of Dhuoda and her contemporaries—Franks, nobles, and women.

The purpose of this translation is to communicate Dhuoda's work to the wider English-speaking audience for whom its potential interest has been demonstrated. The Carolingian author herself hoped her handbook would teach her young son, a beginner, what he needed to know about his ninth-century world. The present translation aims to mirror Dhuoda's intent. Because of its introductory nature, the Frankish woman's book provides much of the information necessary for its effective interpretation even by those previously uninitiated in medieval literature. The author describes for her son the human universe, its relationship with the divine, and the right standards of moral behavior. She discusses the place of study in William's future life—how to read, even how to use her own little book. As she begins and ends her text, she records the conditions under which she has produced it. A modern reader is therefore able, with little further study, to recognize connections among the author's historical circumstances, her social and religious beliefs, and her notion of the place of literature in describing and directing life.

Dhuoda's eloquence, particularly in regard to her historical circumstances, discourages explication of her text. Still, some discussion here of her work's background, sources, and significance for understanding the Carolingian world may be useful, especially for those whose investigation of the early Middle Ages and of Dhuoda's work will not carry them to the handbook's Latin text and to the abundant scholarship on ninth-century life and literature. Some reflection on Dhuoda's thought and presentation may, finally, encourage readers' own interpretations of the position of women among the Carolingian nobility.

The Composition, Sources, and Content of Dhuoda's Handbook

Despite her claim to have written in haste and under duress (10.1), Dhuoda organizes her work according to a coherent plan. The "books" of varying length into which Riché divides her text—sections that neither Dhuoda nor medieval copyists of her text defined but that nevertheless form useful divisions and are in any case standardized by the definitive edition[24]—are therefore maintained in this translation, as follows:

Prologue—the author and her reasons for writing
Book 1—loving God
Book 2—the mystery of Trinity
Book 3—social order and secular success
Book 4—moral life
Book 5—God's chastisement of those he loves
Book 6—the usefulness of the beatitudes
Book 7—the deaths of the body and of the spirit
Book 8—how to pray and for whom
Book 9—interpreting numbers
Book 10—summary of the work's major points, more on the author
Book 11—the usefulness of reciting the Psalms

These books follow one another in a loosely but sensibly connected fashion. Dhuoda offers opening remarks about her intentions for her work and about her and William's circumstances (Prologue), then begins in earnest by instructing her son on the fundamentals of religion (Books 1, 2). She continues with advice on conduct in secular life (the long books: 3, 4). She adds a variety of sometimes sobering, sometimes comforting evidence for the connection between heavenly and earthly existence and discusses the way in which prayer and reading of scriptural texts can fend off secular evils (the short books: 5, 6, 7, 8, 9). Finally, Dhuoda makes a verse summary of the material she has presented, appending a few further autobiographical passages (Book 10). Reluctant to set aside her work, she then resumes a discussion of psalm-reading for spiritual advancement and at last takes her leave of the reader (Book 11).

The comprehensive theme of Dhuoda's handbook for her son's religious life and his conduct as a secular nobleman is the relationship between temporal and eternal life, how William should understand God's precepts for a Christian nobleman and how these will guide him to heaven. In her development of this broad topic, Dhuoda freely —even proudly—asserts, she has borrowed heavily from books she knows, choosing ideas and passages that she believes, through her knowledge of her son's world as well as of his youthful interests, will be most useful to his learning.[25]

Riché's edition of Dhuoda's handbook identifies her clear familiarity with works of Alcuin of York, the leading thinker of Charlemagne's court, and her probable knowledge of texts of other eighth- and ninth-century intellectuals, such as Ambrosius Autpertus, Jonas of Orléans, Paulinus of Aquileia, Rabanus Maurus, and Lupus of Ferrières. Among older texts, the works of Isidore of Seville, Venantius Fortunatus, and Gregory of Tours are used by Dhuoda. She likewise knows various descriptions of monastic life, most importantly the Rule of Benedict of Nursia. Among the Latin Fathers, the preeminent founders of Christian doctrine in late antiquity, Augustine of Hippo is most familiar to her, but she also refers directly to Gregory the Great. In a few instances, she mentions the lives of saints.[26]

Dhuoda is, then, widely read in such Christian texts as were available in monastic libraries of her period and as Alcuin had chosen as basic to the education of lay nobles in the palace school at Aachen. How many of these works were at hand as she gathered the materials for her handbook for William is unclear from the text because she quotes loosely, frequently from memory. Despite the breadth of her Christian erudition, however, Dhuoda seems to know only grammatical texts from among pagan classical authors. As Riché has argued, the general shape of her literary background accurately reflects the education typical of the palace schools for nobility under Charlemagne and his successor.[27]

Dhuoda's education, like the learning of other lay nobles, centered on the Vulgate Bible. This text, in Alcuin's redaction, overwhelms the Carolingian lady's other sources in both the frequency and the familiarity of her reference to it.[28] Dhuoda constantly quotes from and alludes to both testaments but strongly favors the Old Testament. She refers to Psalms far more than any other book and shows special attention to the scriptural record of David, the king of Israel, whom she accepts as the author of them all.[29]

The Carolingian author had some assistance, surely from a priest or a monk, in the compilation of her work. She occasionally mentions that she is "having copied out" for William one or another piece of borrowed advice (3.8; 9.1). Indeed, it has been proposed that Dhuoda made little independent contribution to the text and that a cleric in her household wove together and elaborated on source materials in her name.[30] The highly emotional, autobiographical nature of the handbook's text undercuts any such argument. Although Dhuoda's book, like most medieval works, is strongly grounded in written authority, it is emphatically her own.

Among the handbook's many sources are other guides for moral improvement. Dhuoda's work belongs, like these, to the long-lived genre of the enchiridion or *speculum*, the moral handbook or mirror.[31] In her prologue, she explores the etymology of *manualis*, Latin for the Greek *encheiridion*. Dhuoda explains to William that a little book such as hers is portable or, in a usage closer to her own, handy. She advises her son to employ it as a mirror for his own actions, and she compares the boy's future use of her handbook to the way in which women search in the fuzzy polished-tin reflection of contemporary mirrors for literal blemishes (prol.). The comparison is both homely and witty, but she means with it to plant her work firmly in the distinguished tradition of such texts as Augustine's *Enchiridion on Faith, Hope, and Love*, one of her book's principal models. Works in the same genre by Alcuin, Jonas of Orléans, and Paulinus of Aquileia are likewise familiar to her. But despite her indebtedness to them, and despite the clear links between her perspective and those of other Carolingian authors, Dhuoda's enchiridion is distinctive.[32]

Dhuoda's Moral Perspective

Reflecting her own lay status, Dhuoda confidently asserts the positive spiritual value of ordinary secular activity, of marriage and family life (4.6) as well as leadership and charity in Christian society (4.8). Lay existence, she suggests to her son, is as direct a path to salvation as clerical or monastic life. If William follows his mother's bidding, his actions will be informed by the moral objectives and religious practices prescribed by contemporary clerics—even to the point that he will customarily perform aspects of the *opus Dei*, the office based on the recitation of Psalms, typical of Benedictine monasteries.[33] William's life as a warrior and, his mother hopes, as a father will nevertheless achieve a dignity separate from that of contemporary bishops and monks.

xvii

In Dhuoda's view, William's religious activity will continually remind him throughout his career as a warrior and counselor of kings that pride rooted in secular success is vain and that earthly honor is transient (1.5). To be sure, she also urges that God favors his best servants with earthly rewards (3.3). For Dhuoda, heavenly and earthly order are indeed harmonious; their consonance is evinced in the paternal authority governing both. As God the Father holds sway over creation, so fatherly power should be supreme on earth (2.2; 3.1). Thus Dhuoda begins her third book, her essay on her son's secular status and activity: "Now I must do my best to guide you in how you should fear, love, and be faithful to your lord and father, Bernard, in all things, both when you are with him and when you are apart from him."

Throughout her discussion of social organization, Dhuoda drums into her young son the divine basis of paternal authority. Playing, curiously, on a reverse etymology, she points out that a father's authority is like an abbot's; in the language of the monastic founder Benedict, she urges her son, "listen carefully" to the "instructions . . . of a father" (3.1). Dhuoda treats William's obligation to the king in less emphatic terms—to render good counsel, to act prudently, not unquestioningly to obey the royal command (3.5). Almost as an afterthought, the mother recommends that her son honor priests (3.11). They are God's representatives, but young William's deference to them is a far lesser obligation than his devotion to the patrilineage. "As for you, my son, believe in God, fear him, and love him" (3.5). "Then love, fear, and cherish your father" (3.2). Dhuoda's choice of the language of the Decalogue[34] is more than a commonplace; it is freighted with her conviction that the foundations of human harmony laid in the Old Testament are imperiled in her own generation.

The central point of Dhuoda's argument is that all right social behavior is modeled on the worship of God—hardly a novel notion, but one Dhuoda develops in her own way. According to her, the Father's authority in Trinity is mirrored in the earthly patriarchy of the lineage, not of the kingdom. Worship of God comes first, then obedience to Bernard of Septimania—Dhuoda's husband and William's father. Only afterward should her son consider his obligation to Charles the Bald, his king and lord, and only after that his respect for the priestly class. God the Father and earthly fathers stand as analogues, the ordering functions in Dhuoda's and—she hopes—young William's worlds. The author asserts that in her times such an understanding of right order has fallen prey to the ambitions generated by the contest for empire. Many forget, she points out, that the father comes before the king.[35] Ironically, perhaps, young William here heeded his mother's admonition in a way contrary to her purposes when he rebelled against Charles the Bald for his father's sake and so was killed. Dhuoda means instead that if the clear lines of obligation she describes are maintained, there can be no conflict such as the war between Lothar, Louis the German, and Charles the Bald.

Such an argument is naive. Dhuoda tailors it to William's immaturity, but she herself cannot be so unsophisticated. Her *Handbook* for her son is grounded in the same biblical, moral, and exegetical texts that formed the curriculum of the palace schools. The children of the Carolingian nobility—the daughters perhaps more than the sons[36]— were taught as Dhuoda had been and as she surely had been teaching William since he was a small boy. Dhuoda has, then, selected here for her children those relatively few notions and texts she considers of paramount importance for them. The lessons she offers, supported by an anthology of scriptural and other authoritative quotations, are ones familiar to her elder son. She is as much collecting ideas she has already taught him, of which she now reminds him, as she is offering new thoughts (prol. ["Here begins"]; 10.1).

In this gathering of fundamental teachings, Dhuoda responds to the turmoil of her own and now of her sons' lives by emphasizing to her young reader a simple, family-centered understanding of right order. She places this against the more complex model with which she was familiar through her own education and experience, of which Alcuin—some of whose work Dhuoda knew well—had been an architect, and with which William was certainly presented by his new circumstances. When she minimizes kingly and priestly power, Dhuoda is articulating a standard for social and moral behavior fundamentally different from that typically offered in clerical handbooks for lay performance or from that developed in court ideology since at least Charlemagne's time.[37] Although Dhuoda owed much to Carolingian and prior moral literature, her book is clearly marked by the perspective of an educated laity.

Dhuoda's Readership and Her Maternal Authority

That perspective is rich, but modern scholarship has generally as-
sumed that the intended audience for Dhuoda's work was extremely
narrow.[38] Without question, young William and his little brother were
the primary audience for their mother's work. The text of the handbook suggests, however, that Dhuoda hoped and even expected that it
would be read by others. The author says, in her injunction to William
that he use her book carefully, that it may come into the hands of
others of the young men around him. "I ask of you, and I humbly suggest to your noble youth—just as if I were with you in person—and to
those to whom you may offer this little book for perusal, that they not
condemn me or hold it against me that I am so rash as to take upon
myself so lofty and perilous a task as to speak to you about God" (1.1).

The companions with whom Dhuoda anticipated that her son
would share the work are here unidentified, but further characteristics of her text suggest whom she had in mind. Throughout—and in
this choice she is naturally directed by the shape of her predominantly
Old Testament source material, which is not to say she might not
have expressed a different emphasis—Dhuoda chooses examples from
the histories of kings to explain how fathers and sons, overlords and
underlings, should comport themselves toward each other. She comments, for instance: "Nor should I fail to mention the tree of Absalom,
who rebelled against his father and whom a base death brought to a
sudden fall. Hung from an oak and pierced by lances, he ended his
earthly life in the flower of his youth, with a groan of anguish" (3.1).
Dhuoda's reference to David's son's rebellion, although it might be
understood as a warning to any son who abuses his father's love, is
an especially strong suggestion of the outcome of filial impiety in a
royal house.

Dhuoda's own son has, at her writing, recently been sent to join
the retinue of a prince whose recent family history is hardly less an-
guished than that of the house of David. Much of what she says about
family relations and political connections is as directly applicable to
Charles and his other retainers as it is to her son William. Naturally,
Dhuoda could not have been certain that her son, the young king's
companion, would have wished or dared to share his mother's book
with his lord and his fellows in arms. She was nevertheless aware

that the enchiridion genre in which she wrote was conventionally addressed to magnates rather than boys.[39] Dhuoda's book was certainly for William, but apparently not only for him. If Dhuoda indeed sought a wider audience, the handbook's content must be evaluated in that light.

Modern scholars have consistently interpreted Dhuoda's work as intensely private and unambitious.[40] Dhuoda's self-presentation has, to an extent, lent support to their belief that she expected only her family to know her work. She continually protests her unworthiness to address the moral, theological, and political topics that she in fact takes up with sensitivity and sophistication. Again and again she describes herself as "fragile," lamenting the thinness of her knowledge and the weakness of her intellect (prol.; 10.3). On one occasion she refers to herself, switching the gender of a biblical passage, as a little bitch licking up theological crumbs (1.2).

Although medievalists are accustomed to identifying protestations of incapacity like Dhuoda's as empty conventions,[41] they have in her case found a plausible background to her self-minimization in her presentation of family structures in Frankish society. On its most obvious level, *Handbook for William* advocates thoroughgoing patriarchy in the private, public, and religious contexts alike. When Dhuoda takes up her discussion of worldly order, she begins, "Now I must do my best to guide you in how you should fear, love, and be faithful to your lord and father, Bernard, in all things, both when you are with him and when you are apart from him" (3.1). But just as Dhuoda's protestations of ignorance and illiteracy are incompatible with the shape of her literary remains, so too her assertion that the father is utterly responsible for his son's welfare is incongruous in the contexts of her and William's personal experience and of her own forceful approach to her absent child's education.

Dhuoda's text therefore challenges its readers to unravel its meaning, rather than simplistically to accept its patriarchal posture. Dhuoda is, after all, writing a book of maternal advice for a young son, not a book explicitly revealing the self-perception of the Carolingian nobility or of Carolingian laywomen. In the course of reading the text Dhuoda has prepared, William will inevitably be informed about his own and his fellow nobles' duties. On the other hand, the book is the literary product of his mother's fourteen years of actively rearing her young son in religious, social, and emotional life. The reality of Dhuoda's educative role underlies—to an extent belies—the frequently apologetic manner she adopts as the handbook's author.

Dhuoda's Understanding of Christian Society

Dhuoda tells William on several occasions that her handbook for him is only a small book, a boy's book, and not at all the sort of work she would write for a mature son (10.1). In her statement that her text is a little work for beginners, she again calls to mind Benedict's Rule (3.1).[42] The Carolingian reform that has shaped her education, like that of her contemporaries generally, has tended to blur the line between lay and monastic life, encouraging nobles such as herself and William to order their lives according to a text-based regimen. As Dhuoda exhorts her son to fill his life with the reading and the imitation of Christian texts, she chooses scriptural examples appropriate to his age and station. These examples shed light on Dhuoda's central concerns in gathering her handbook for William. Her choice of scriptural images suggests that Dhuoda intends criticism, more than representation, of the structure of contemporary Frankish society.

Dhuoda's use of the biblical account of David's kingship in Israel, her most richly developed discussion of a scriptural story, is basic to her treatment of familial, social, and political order. Dhuoda recalls how Saul lost power and how David grieved over the deaths of the king and of Jonathan, as well as how David's own rule was marred by the rebellion of Absalom. When she invokes David's lament for Saul and his son, she borrows his eloquent grief with apparent reference to the fratricidal disruption of her own Frankish world: "How are the valiant fallen in battle, [and] the weapons of war perished?" "I grieve for thee, my brother Jonathan, . . . amiable to me above the love of women" (3.8).[43]

Dhuoda's examination of this preeminent scriptural instance of father-son and king-subject inversion suggests that she saw relations among her own people as utterly disordered. When she proposes rigid adherence to paternal interests as the solution to this disastrous situation, she effectively offers a radical solution. Her theory has simple, compelling implications. If everyone obeys his father and if the father

obeys his lord and if both attend to priestly advice, the many antago-
nistic forces among the central-ninth-century nobility will be locked
into a neatly hierarchical and fully peaceful configuration (10.2). The
sons of Louis the Pious will keep peace according to their late father's
dispensation; Bernard of Septimania will serve Charles the Bald and
ensure the future of his son William among the king's counselors; and
David and Absalom will not again come to grief.

Dhuoda never asserts that exclusive patriarchal allegiance is a
reality but only proposes an ideal. Her urgency that William obey first
his father, then his earthly lord, and then the priesthood grows from
the violence of her historical circumstances. Dhuoda's essay on the
family and the nobility is thus normative, not descriptive. Although
the lives of Frankish nobles were frequently disrupted, the years in
which Dhuoda wrote were, for people like herself, exceptional in their
destructiveness. Everything that William's mother wrote to her son is
colored by this circumstance.

When Dhuoda therefore portrays an ideal social order as one in
which the son's welfare depends absolutely on his obedience to his
father, she certainly says what she means, and what she says is in general harmony with much else that we know of heredity and authority
in the Carolingian empire.[44] On the other hand, the vehemence of her
argument compels interpretive attention. When Dhuoda appeals for
the integrity of patrilineal kinship ties over all other forms of noble
allegiance, she oversteps herself. Clearly she fears that William may
be shaken in his loyalty to his father when he joins the retinue of
Charles the Bald—as he might wisely have been, given the vicissi-
tudes of Bernard of Septimania's own allegiances and fortunes.[45] Her
eagerness for William to cling to his own family suggests less that
strict patrilineal connections were maintained among nobles of her
generation than that even family connections were endangered by the
contemporary crisis of the empire.

Dhuoda's use of many other scriptural texts reveals that the Carolingian author's understanding of human relations was richly tex-
tured and was informed by an original, identifiably lay reading of
scriptures bearing on the organization of the Christian community.
Despite Dhuoda's preference for Old Testament quotations, her faith
is thoroughly New Testament in its sensibility; she sees love, *cari-*

tas, as the fundamental link among human beings.[46] So, for instance, Dhuoda uses the scriptural image of harts crossing a stream to describe human interdependence, writing: "The harts have such intelligence and such commensurate discretion that, when they perceive that the one in front is weakening, the leader becomes a follower and eventually the last in line so that the others may assist and support him; then they choose another to go first. Thus, as one individual takes the place of another, each feels the brotherly fellowship of love run through them all" (3.10).

Dhuoda's vision of social order is not, then, unrelievedly patriarchal but is complex, the expression of educated lay spirituality as well as tradition and experience as a member of the Carolingian elite. Even male ecclesiastics such as Jonas of Orléans acknowledged that Carolingian women had an essential role in moral and religious education.[47] Dhuoda, in assuming educative responsibility in so active a fashion as to write a book for her son in a genre made up chiefly by the works of ecclesiastics for lay magnates, asserts this maternal prerogative. Her text portrays its author as part of the family into which she has married, and adds her own considerable learning and authority to that of William's patrilineage. Although she reminds her son to take heed for the souls of his father's family (10.5),[48] her own soul is the one she most urgently exhorts him to remember (10.4). At the same time, Dhuoda emphasizes to her son that she speaks "as your mother," and therefore with unquestioned influence, about his spiritual life, moral behavior, and activity as a noble warrior (prol. ["Here begins"]).

The question then arises whether Dhuoda's self-perception—and the self-perception of Carolingian lay noblewomen, to the extent that we can generalize from her presentation—is simply paradoxical: she advocates a glorification of the male lineage and nevertheless athletically interposes herself in the shaping of her son's life in the male worlds of battlefield and council. But such a conclusion is jarring and unnecessary. Dhuoda's forthrightness and conviction in her address to William and to young men like him proceed from her certainty of her fitness to serve as his adviser. In part this certainty grows from her own education and experience, and in part from her awareness that her marriage has effectively joined her to the lineage that she now holds up as a paradigm for good social order. As Dhuoda sees it, maternal authority and patriarchal organization are mutually supportive, even mutually necessary.

This observation about Dhuoda's views does not transform the import of the many other sources for the family relationships of the Carolingian nobility. There is no question that the world of Dhuoda was one in which women's direct political and economic power was less than it had been before Charlemagne's time, under the Merovingian dynasty.[49] The significance of Dhuoda's commentary on family structures concerns the way in which contemporary women perceived their status among their fathers, husbands, brothers, and sons. *Handbook for William* is evidence that ninth-century Frankish women retained powerful influence within their families.

The Carolingian nobility would be the last laity for many generations to be educated at a level to have produced or appreciated Dhuoda's work, so we should not find it surprising that few medieval copies survive. Nor is it surprising that when we hear the single voice of a thoughtful laywoman of the early Middle Ages, it is a voice of Dhuoda's generation. But neither the uniqueness of her text nor the self-effacement of her presentation should obscure Dhuoda's assumption that the males of her family would be guided by her forceful direction.

This woman author's attempt to set her son's thinking right is more extraordinary for its challenge to her generation's general pessimism than for its assertion of maternal authority within a noble lineage. When Dhuoda sent her work to her son, she was apprehensive about his future but determined to persuade him and his companions to restore order among their troubled people. Only a few months later Nithard, the only other lay author of Dhuoda's generation from whose pen a substantial work survives, closed the fourth book of his histories of the Carolingian civil wars: "Each goes his separate way, dissension and struggle abound. Once there was abundance and happiness everywhere, now everywhere is want and sadness."[50] So dire a description of the central ninth century was clearly to Nithard's rhetorical purposes as he ended his account of the conflict among the sons of Louis the Pious, but it was historically accurate. The next decades bore out the historian's foreboding and the mother's fears, bringing the eclipse of that Carolingian revival of learning to which both their works pertain.

The Manuscripts, the Riché Edition, and the Present Translation

This English translation of Dhuoda's *Handbook for William* is based directly on the Riché edition. Unaware of the imminent publication of Riché's edition in the distinguished series Sources Chrétiennes, Myra Ellen Bowers, a doctoral student at Catholic University, edited and translated another version, available only from University Microfilms.[51] Although Bowers's version offers some better readings than Riché's[52] and is accompanied by a closely literal translation apparently intended to illuminate difficult passages rather than to make Dhuoda's work available to a non-Latinist readership,[53] an English translation such as this one should offer its audience easy reference to the standard, widely available edition. The present translation's indebtedness to Bowers's dissertation therefore is limited to occasional reference to her Latin text and to her introductory essay, especially valuable for its emphasis on Dhuoda's proximity to Benedictine education and spirituality.[54]

In general, the translation below attempts to render Dhuoda's straightforward, emotionally laden prose in corresponding English. This has not always been easy. The Carolingian author's style has been criticized as inept; her text is often rambling, sometimes difficult to follow, and filled with small inelegancies such as pleonasm and grammatical imprecision.[55] She shares with many of her contemporaries a predilection for mingling a variety of verse forms, including acrostic poems; she lacks skill in versification, and it is difficult to tell even whether her Latin meter is intended as rhythmic or quantitative.[56]

As Riché argues, however, Dhuoda's deviation from the classicizing style of contemporary clerics shows much about the slow transformation of Latin into Romance. Her written language is closer to the spoken vernacular of her times than to the classicizing Latin of the great majority of Carolingian literary works.[57] The text of Dhuoda's handbook is therefore of philological as much as historical interest. Nor should its literary merit be judged by its failure to mimic the sophistication of clerical compositions. Dhuoda's style effectively serves her intent to engage her reader in her vision of lay experience and to communicate the urgency of her desire for her son's secular prosperity and eternal salvation. The present translation therefore seeks to replicate the strength of Dhuoda's presentation without investing it with an alien smoothness.

The manuscripts of Dhuoda's work all show that its original had some seventy chapters, numbered variously in the surviving copies. The Riché edition arranges these yet again among the books into which he divides the text. Riché's divisions are retained here and numbered after his fashion, along with the chapter headings that he reproduces and for which there is indeed manuscript evidence.[58] Readers interested in Dhuoda's language, grammar, and syntax will wish to consult the Riché edition and the several scholarly responses to his editorial decisions on Dhuoda's spelling, syntax, and usage.[59] Even those whose interest in Dhuoda is limited to reading her handbook in English should, however, be aware of the thinness of her work's manuscript tradition and the difficulty we face in determining exactly what she or her scribe wrote.

Only three medieval or early modern manuscripts of independent value for establishing Dhuoda's text are known to exist. The earliest surviving copy of Dhuoda's work is a late-tenth- or early-eleventh-century manuscript now preserved at Nîmes; this manuscript comprises only nine fragments of the handbook text. A virtually complete seventeenth-century copy of some earlier version of Dhuoda's text, not that now at Nîmes, survives in Paris; this copy has many errors, some of which were corrected in the nineteenth century by Dhuoda's first modern editor, Edouard Bondurand, through collation with the Nîmes manuscript. A fourteenth-century manuscript was much more recently discovered by André Vernet in Barcelona; this manuscript, included in a volume of pedagogical texts, offers virtually the same contents as the Paris copy but was apparently corrected against yet another early copy that is now lost. Riché believes that the Barcelona manuscript of Dhuoda's work, because it has many better readings than the other complete copy and because it appears to have been made within the bounds of Bernard of Septimania's Catalan territories, descends directly from the handbook of the addressee, William. The Riché edition represents all three extant manuscripts, for the most part presenting the readings of the Barcelona copy.[60] Dhuoda's work, like many important medieval texts, has thus survived by slim chance, and many of its passages are obscure because of errors in its transmission. Her handbook is nonetheless fortunate in its editorship by a preeminent scholar of Carolingian letters.

Notes to this translation indicate the few cases where I have opted against Riché's readings or emendations or have departed from his interpretation of the meaning of Dhuoda's text. The notes likewise adopt Riché's identification of the Carolingian author's sources unless stated otherwise, although I have frequently omitted the editor's many references to non-English scholarly publications and his occasional citations of ancient or medieval texts only loosely parallel to Dhuoda's or of strictly philological interest. Riché's illuminating historical commentary is generally reproduced and attributed specifically to him, while fuller historical notes have been added where appropriate for a non-specialist English-speaking audience. The bibliography includes basic elements in relevant foreign-language scholarship but emphasizes English translations and commentary.

Within the text of the following translation, Frankish proper names are adjusted from Dhuoda's Latinizations to the forms conventional in English scholarship on the Carolingian period. Biblical quotations, rendered in italic, follow the Douay translation of the Vulgate, with punctuation adjusted to current American usage.

The Handbook of Dhuoda

SENT TO HER SON WILLIAM

Here begins the text.

The little book before you branches out in three directions. Read it
through and, by the end, you will understand what I mean. I would
like it to be called three things at once, as befits its contents—rule,
model, and handbook.[1] These terms all mirror each other. The rule
comes from me, the model is for you, and the handbook is as much
from me as for you—composed by me, received by you.

For *manus,* "hand," as in "manual" or "handbook," means many
things—sometimes the power of God, sometimes the might of the
Son, and sometimes even the Son himself. It means the power of God
when the Apostle[2] says, *Be ye humbled under the mighty hand of
God.*[3] Or it means the power of the Son when Daniel says, *His power is
an everlasting power.*[4] Or again sometimes it means the Son himself,
as the Psalmist[5] says, *Put forth your hand from on high,*[6] that is your
Son from highest heaven. All these things and similar expressions signify holy action and power, for "hand" means action carried out. As
Scripture says, *the hand of the Lord was upon me,*[7] that is his redemption leading believers to perfection. Again, *the hand of the Lord was
strengthening me,*[8] and again, *for the hand of the Lord was with him.*[9]

As for the suffix *-al,* with which "manual" ends, it has many
meanings too. But in this instance I will use it in three senses, as the
Fathers[10] did. I will use it as destination, perfection, and end.[11] For it
is like the word for "wings," *ales,* which refers to the cock, the messenger of the morning who brings an end to the night and heralds the
daytime hours. For what meaning does this word "manual" have un-

I

less it signifies the end of ignorance? The messenger to which it refers foreknows the light of things to come. It is as if he says, *the night is passed, and the day is at hand.*[12] This cock is Christ, who said, If I am the day and you the hours, follow me.[13]

From the beginning of this book to the end, both in form and in content, in the meter and rhythm of the poetry as well as in the prose passages here—know that everything, through it all, in it all, is intended entirely for you, for the health of your soul and body. I wish that you eagerly take this work in your own hand and fulfill its precepts, after my hand has addressed it to you. I wish you to hold it, turn its pages and read it, so that you may fulfill it in worthy action. For this little model-book, called a handbook, is a lesson from me and a task for you. As someone said, *I have planted, Apollo watered, but God gave the increase.*[14] What further can I say, my son, except that— thinking on your past good deeds—I have in this work *fought the good fight, I have kept the faith, I have finished my course?*[15] And how is what I say of worth unless in him who said, *It is consummated?*[16] For whatever I have accomplished in this volume, from its beginning on, according to the Hebrew speech and to Greek letters and to the Latin language, I have completed in him who is called God.[17]

In the name of Holy Trinity.

In the name of Holy Trinity, here begins the handbook of Dhuoda, which she sent to her son William.[18]

I am well aware that most women rejoice that they are with their children in this world, but I, Dhuoda, am far away from you, my son William. For this reason I am anxious and filled with longing to do something for you. So I send you this little work written down in my name, that you may read it for your education, as a kind of mirror.[19] And I rejoice that, even if I am apart from you in body, the little book before you may remind you, when you read it, of what you should do on my behalf.[20]

Epigraph for the following work.[21]

God, highest creator of light, and author
　Of the heaven and the stars, eternal king, holy one,

In your mercy complete this task begun by me.
    Though I am ignorant, I seek understanding of you,
So that I may know what pleases you
    And, now and in the future, follow the right path.
One and triune in all the universe,
    You grant your servants prosperity through the ages.
You assign just rewards to these men's worthy actions,[22]
    And heavenly honor to those who worship you.
As much as I am able, on bended knee
    I give thanks to you, my maker.
I beseech you to bestow your aid upon me,
    Raising me to heaven on your right side.
For I believe that there, in your kingdom,
    Your servants may forever remain in peace.
Although I am unworthy, weak, and an exile,
    Made of earth, drawn to the lowest depths,
I nevertheless have a friend,[23] my lady-companion,
    Who is sure to set your people free from sin.
You, center who hold the turning of the heaven,
    Who enfold in your hand the land and the sea,[24]
To you I entrust my son William:
    May you ordain that he be prosperous in all things.
May he stay his course at every hour and minute;
    May he love you, his creator, above all.
With your sons may he be worthy
    To ascend to heaven with swift and happy step.
In you may his mind always keep watchful,
    Attentive; may he always live joyously.
When he is wounded, may he never fall into anger
    Nor lose his way from among your servants.
Merry, may he rejoice in a happy path
    And may he arrive above shining in virtue;
May he always seek from you what he ought.
    You who grant without recompense, give him understanding,
That he may know to believe in you, to love you,
    And to praise you who are holy with redoubled thanks.

May your expansive grace come to him,
 Peace and security in body and in mind.
May he flourish with his children in this world,
 But may he have the other world's gifts as well.
May he read and reread this volume from time to time,
 And may the words of the saints shape his thought.[25]
May he draw understanding from you—
 How, when, and to whom he should give aid.
And may he pursue the fourfold virtues assiduously,[26]
 So that he remain capable of many things.
Generous and wise, just and brave,
 May he never abandon moderation.
He will never have another like me,[27]
 Unworthy though I am, but still his mother,
Who always—in every hour and minute—
 Prays to you devotedly: have mercy upon him.
Many storms of troubles beset me
 As I struggle for him with my feeble strength.
To you, who are the source of all bounty,
 I entrust him, in all that he does giving thanks to you.
Although there may be discord in the kingdom and the fatherland,
 You alone remain unchanging.
Whether worthy men seek fitting ends or not,
 All depends on your judgment.
Yours is the kingdom and yours the power,[28]
 Yours the universal governance of the earth,[29]
And to you alone all things are subject.
 You who reign always, have mercy on my children.

May he and his brother—my two sons born to this existence—
Live long, I pray you, and may they always love you.

Reader, if you desire to know the key,
 Look at the beginning of each verse.
Then, passing through swiftly, you may see
 What it is that I have written.
I, mother of two boys,
 Ask that you pray to the gracious creator

That he raise these children's father up to heaven
And join me with them in God's kingdom.

Begin reading at the first letter of the first verse and continue to the first letter of the last.[30] So my poem ends. With Christ's help I now undertake the work I have begun for my children.

Here begins the prologue.

Things that are obvious to many people often escape me. Those who are like me lack understanding and have dim insight, but I am even less capable than they.[31] Yet always there is he at my side who *opened the mouths of the dumb, and made the tongues of infants eloquent.*[32] I, Dhuoda, despite my weakness of mind, unworthy as I am among worthy women—I am still your mother, my son William, and it is to you that I now address the words of my handbook. From time to time children are fascinated by dice more than all the other games that they enjoy. And sometimes women are absorbed in examining their faces in mirrors,[33] in order then to cover their blemishes and be more beautiful, for the worldly intention of pleasing their husbands. I hope that you may bring the same care, burdened though you may be by the world's pressures, to reading this little book addressed to you by me. For my sake, attend to it—according to my jest—as children do to their dice or women to their mirrors.

Even if you eventually have many more books, read this little work of mine often. May you, with God's help, be able to understand it to your own profit. You will find in it all you may wish to know in compact form. You will find in it a mirror in which you can without hesitation contemplate the health of your soul, so that you may be pleasing not only in this world, but to him who formed you out of dust.[34] What is essential, my son William, is that you show yourself to be such a man on both levels that you are both effective in this world and pleasing to God in every way.[35]

My great concern, my son William, is to offer you helpful words. My burning, watchful heart especially desires that you may have in this little volume what I have longed to be written down for you, about how you were born through God's grace. I shall best begin there.

Preface.

In the eleventh year of the imperial rule of our lord Louis, who then reigned by Christ's favor—on the twenty-ninth of June 824—I was given in marriage at the palace of Aachen to my lord Bernard, your father, to be his legitimate wife.[36] It was still in that reign, in its thirteenth year on the twenty-ninth of November,[37] that with God's help, as I believe, you were born into this world, my firstborn and much-desired son.

Afterward, as the wretchedness of this world grew and worsened, in the midst of the many struggles and disruptions in the kingdom,[38] that emperor followed the path common to all men. For in the twenty-eighth year of his reign, he paid the debt of his earthly existence before his time.[39] In the year after his death, your brother was born on the twenty-second of March in the city of Uzès.[40] This child, born after you, was the second to come forth from my body by God's mercy. He was still tiny and had not yet received the grace of baptism when Bernard, my lord and the father of you both, had the baby brought to him in Aquitaine in the company of Elefantus, bishop of Uzès, and others of his retainers.[41]

Now I have been away from you for a long time, for my lord constrains me to remain in this city. Nonetheless I applaud his success.[42] But, moved by longing for both of you, I have undertaken to have this little book—a work on the scale of my small understanding—copied down and sent to you. Although I am besieged by many troubles, may this one thing be God's will, if it please him—that I might see you again with my own eyes. I would think it certain that I would, if God were to grant me some virtue. But since salvation is far from me, sinful woman that I am,[43] I only wish it, and my heart grows weak in this desire.[44]

As for you, I have heard that your father, Bernard, has given you as a hostage to the lord king Charles.[45] I hope that you acquit yourself of this worthy duty with perfect good will. Meanwhile, as Scripture says, *Seek ye therefore the kingdom of God . . . and all these things shall be added unto you,*[46] that is all that is necessary for the enjoyment of your soul and your body.

So the preface comes to an end.

Book One

1. *On loving God.*

God must be loved and praised—not only by powers on high, but also by every human creature who walks upon the earth and reaches toward heaven. I beseech you, my son, since you are among these, always to try your best to find the way to climb to its secure height along with those others who are worthy and who are able to love God. Then, along with them, you will be able to reach his kingdom without end.[1]

I ask of you, and I humbly suggest to your noble youth—just as if I were with you in person—and to those to whom you may offer this little book for perusal,[2] that they not condemn me or hold it against me that I am so rash as to take upon myself so lofty and perilous a task as to speak to you about God. Indeed, knowing my human frailty,[3] I never cease to chastise myself, *whereas I am* wretched, *dust and ashes.*[4] And what shall I say? If the patriarchs and prophets and the other saints, from the first-made man up until now, have been unable to understand entirely the accounts of holy mysteries, how much less should I be able to—I who am but weak, born of a lowly people?[5] And if, as Scripture says, *the heaven of heavens cannot contain thee*[6] on account of your greatness, Lord, what can I, unlearned as I am, say about you?

We read in Genesis that when the blessed Moses, in the course of his direct conversation with God, wished to look upon God's countenance, he said to the Lord, *If . . . I have found favor in thy sight, shew me thy face, that I may know thee.*[7] The Lord replied to him, *Thou canst not see my face, for man shall not see me* and be able to live.[8] If it was so for the saints, what do you think about those on earth who are like me? But because God commands that he not be seen, my spirit falters, for my desire is burning.

2. *On seeking God.*

You and I must seek God out, my son; we take our existence from his approval, *we live, and move, and are.*[9] Even I, unworthy and frail as a shadow, seek him as best I can and unceasingly call upon his aid as best I know and understand it. It is absolutely necessary for me to do so in all things. For it often happens that an insistent little bitch, scrambling under the master's table with the male puppies, is able to snatch up and eat such crumbs as fall.[10] He who makes the mouth of a dumb beast to speak and opens my understanding,[11] giving me insight[12] according to his ancient mercy, is indeed a powerful Lord; he prepares for his faithful *a table in the wilderness,*[13] giving them *their measure of wheat* to fill them.[14] That Lord can fulfill even the will of me his servant, if he so wishes. At least under his table—that is, within his holy church—I can see from afar the puppies who are the ministers of his holy altars, and can gather words for both you and me, my son William—clear, worthy, beautiful words from among their intellectual and spiritual crumbs. For I know *his commiserations have not failed.*[15]

In the past and in the present, and even in the future, the Lord is here and everywhere, and he has the power to do all good. It is in his nature always to exist, as he says, *I am Alpha and Omega.*[16] And *I am who am.*[17] Scripture says again, *He who is, hath sent me to you,*[18] and so forth.

3. *On God's greatness.*

God is great and sublime, my son William, for he *looketh on the low, and the high*—that is, the proud—*he knoweth afar off.*[19] Frail man raises himself up, but God in heaven is still far above him.[20] But then the Lord descends to man, humbling himself, gracious. Therefore, humble yourself often so that you may be exalted by him forever.[21] For he knows of what formless matter you and I are made.[22] As Scripture says: the Lord's eyes saw, and *God looked down from heaven on the children of men: to see if there were any that did understand, or did seek* him.[23]

The Lord "saw our actions in the first half-light,"[24] that is *from the rising of the sun unto the going down of the same.*[25] Or he saw them from our birth to the moment of our death, or again "in the first half-light," that is, from the shaping of the first man, Adam, up until that last man to be born and to die at the end of the world.[26] He knows whatever human weakness ponders, speaks of, or does. Among men he *knoweth who are his,*[27] bringing them from the depths to heaven, granting them his kingdom and rewarding them as they deserve in their struggle for good.

4. *On God's sublimity.*

As for God's sublimity and greatness, my son, as Paul the Apostle says, no mortal man has ever been or will ever be able to understand it fully. For Paul says: *O the depth of the riches of the wisdom and of the knowledge of God! How incomprehensible are his judgments, and how unsearchable his ways!*[28] And again: *For who hath known the mind of the Lord? Or who hath been his counsellor?*[29] *For who in the clouds can be compared to the Lord: or who . . . shall be like to God?*[30] You know the answer: none. Why? Because *thou only knowest the hearts of the children of men,*[31] and thou art *the most high Lord over all the earth.*[32]

Still, although I am as weak as a shadow, I must bring to your awareness, my son William, what you can understand of God above. For I neither can nor have the strength to nor should set forth for you a complete discourse. Instead, I now begin my partial attempt at such a task, putting together those things that are most important to understand.

5. *More on the same topic. On God.*

A certain learned man—O, how great are his merits!—says, "In the name God, *Deus,* there are two syllables and four letters."[33] When you find these things out and read them, what is there to say but that the very word God contains a great and wondrous mystery? Now, as one of the fools,[34] let me begin with the first letter, which—even by itself—reveals much of importance in its two forms.

Our *D*, with which the name of God begins, is called *delta* by the Greeks. Thus it signifies four, the number of perfection, in Greek numerals; according to the Latin language, the same *D* expands to contain the great number 500. Nor is this empty of holy mystery.[35]

One, two, three, and four—although they each have independent meaning—amount to other numbers in combination. All these things are set forth clearly by learned scholars: five times five is twenty-five; and twice that amounts to fifty. Five, fifty, five hundred.

Either interpretation, the Latin or the Greek, contains all those things that are appropriate to say of him who is called God. The number five offers a reminder of the five senses of the body, that is, sight, hearing, taste, smell, and touch. The number four refers to various groups of four—on the one hand the four characteristics of bodies, that is, hot, cold, wet, and dry; or the four virtues, that is, justice, strength, wisdom, and moderation; or the words of the four evangelists. Or this four means or refers to the four directions in the universe, that is, east, west, north, and south. As for the number three, it contains the perfect trinity seen in the highest God—Father, Son, and Holy Spirit; or there are also the three gifts, all from him who is called God, that is, pure thought, holy speech, and perfect action. And as for the number two, there are the two lives, the active and the contemplative,[36] or the two powers, thought and action, that depend on the two commandments to love God and neighbor. But the number one, which comes before them all—understand it to signify him who is called God.

I direct you always to ponder in your heart the words of the holy gospels and the writings of the other Fathers in respect to the virtues, the elements, and the senses of the body, so that in thinking, speaking, and acting well you may believe that he who is called God endures endlessly as one in trinity and three in oneness. None can know his greatness. It is he, as Scripture says, whom *the morning stars . . . praised together* with *all the sons of God.*[37] It is he who *laid the foundations of the earth*[38] and *the measures thereof,*[39] who *shut up the sea with doors,*[40] and *made a cloud the garment thereof.*[41] If he indeed is such and if he rules all these things throughout time, he can bring you too to the height of perfection, my beloved son William; he can nourish you and cause you to become great. When you begin to consider who the Lord is, how great, and of what character, and when you then cannot comprehend him or find any help such as he, then you will truly know that he is God. As a certain poet says, "he gave his commands and things were created, he spoke and they were made—the heaven and the earth, the depths of the sea, the globes of the sun and the moon."[42]

In this world we speak as though everything is under our own power, but this is not so. A certain individual, for instance, is embroiled in this world and says of it, This is my kingdom and "in all my kingdom," without thinking that *the kingdom is the Lord's*,[43] and all things that live in it. Even Nebuchadnezzar, an evil unbeliever, said after he had been overwhelmed to prostration and then to a degree had recovered: the Lord is the king who rules and reigns, who has the power to raise up and to humble those who exalt themselves in pride. It is the Lord to whom reign belongs, and he will give it out to whomever he wishes.[44] Another man who is embroiled here too may say, "this land is mine," and not keep in mind the saying of the Psalmist, *the earth is the Lord's.*[45] *The birds are the Lord's*, and also *the fishes* that leap and *pass through the paths of the sea.*[46] For *in his hand are all the ends of the earth*,[47] and it is he who rules and gives order to all things dwelling in it. Embroiled as we are in the temporal world, we say and they say, "This is mine, all these things." They say that it is, but it is not. They have it, and they do not have it—or they have it only for a short time but not always. They have it for a time, not for all time.

I think about such things as I have heard read. And I have even seen some of my and your relatives, my son, who had the appearance of power in the secular world, but are not powerful now. Perhaps they are still mighty before God because of their worthy merits, but they are no longer powerful in the physical world, in their action here. For these and for others I ask on my knees that there be eternal rest. As for me, although I am the least of those who think upon the fact of man's mortality and what follows it, I see what is to come.

Therefore, we must fear and love the Lord, and we must believe steadfastly in his immortality. It is he who is always, without any diminution, the powerful king ruling and doing whatever he sees fit, for all things are beneath his will and power. *There is none that can resist thy will*[48] by saying: why have you done this? He is the God of all; his is the power and the kingdom and the rule. The holy man Daniel said confidently of this Lord's power and kingdom, *his power is an everlasting power that shall not be taken away: and his kingdom that shall not be destroyed,*[49] and much more.

6. Moral interpretation.

What shall I, fragile vessel that I am, say further? Soon I will join the majority as their companion.[50] But indeed, if heaven and the expanse of the earth were stretched through the air like a leaf of parchment,[51] if the furrows of the sea were changed into firm earth, and if all those who have been born into this world to plow its entire surface had been learned writers through some increase in the capacity of the human race, although such would have been contrary to nature—even so many learned people would not have been able to comprehend the greatness and the breadth and the height and the sublimity of the omnipotent Lord, or to tell the divinity, knowledge, goodness, and mercy of him who is called God. Since he is such and so great that none can understand his being, I beseech you to fear and love him with all your heart, all your spirit, and all your understanding. Wherever you are, whatever you do, bless him and sing, *for he is good, and his mercy endureth for ever.*[52]

Believe that he is above, below, within, and without; for he is higher, deeper, inside, and outside.[53] He is above in that he oversees and rules us. He is "high," and as the Psalmist says, *his glory* is *above the heavens.*[54] He is below, for he supports us all: *in him we live, and move, and are,*[55] and we exist in him always. He is within, for he fills and satisfies us with his good things, as is written: *the earth shall be filled with the fruit of thy works;*[56] and thou *fillest with blessing every living creature.*[57] He is outside, for he surrounds us with an impregnable wall, fortifies us, protects and defends us, as is written: he girds us with a wall and puts on his crown like a shield.[58] I, your mother, although I may be worthless in the smallness and the shallowness of my understanding—I believe that he who is God is such, and is blessed for all time. Amen.

7. Cautionary words on the same topic.

And so I urge you, O my handsome and beloved son William, that you not be distracted by the mundane cares of this earthly world from acquiring many volumes. In these books you should seek out and learn from the wise men of the church, the holiest of masters, more and greater things about God your creator than are written here. Beseech the Lord, cherish him, and love him. If you do this, he will be your guardian, your leader, your companion, and your country—*the way, and the truth, and the life*[59]—endowing you most generously with prosperity in this world. He will bring all your enemies to peace. As for you, as is written in Job, *Gird up thy loins like a man.*[60] Be humble of heart and chaste in body. *Set thyself up on high, and be glorious,* and *clothe thyself with beauty.*[61]

What more can I say? I, Dhuoda, am always with you to encourage you. In the future, should I fail you by my absence, you have this little moral work as a reminder, so that as you read in spirit and body and as you pray to God you may be able to look upon me as if in a mirror.[62] Then you may clearly see your duty to me. My son, my firstborn son— you will have other teachers to present you with works of fuller and richer usefulness, but not anyone like me, your mother, whose heart burns on your behalf.

Read the words I address to you, understand them and fulfill them in action. And when your little brother, whose name I still do not know, has received the grace of baptism in Christ, do not hesitate to teach him, to educate him, to love him, and to call him to progress from good to better. When the time has come that he has learned to speak and to read, show him this little volume gathered together into a handbook by me and written down in your name. Urge him to read it, for he is your flesh and your brother.[63] I, your mother Dhuoda, urge you, as if I even now spoke to both of you, that you "hold up your heart" from time to time when you are oppressed by the troubles of this world, and "look upon him who reigns in heaven"[64] and is called God. May that all-powerful one whom I mention frequently even in my unworthiness make both of you, my sons—along with my lord and master Bernard, your father—happy and joyful in the present world. May he make you successful in all your undertakings, and after the end of this life may he bring you rejoicing to heaven among his saints. Amen.

Book Two

1. *On Trinity.*

Holy Trinity, my son, is the Father and the Son and the Holy Spirit, for so we read.[1] I neither presume—nor am able—to write for you what I might in the section of my little book on this topic. Read the volumes of the orthodox Fathers, and you will discover what Trinity is. Then when you find an explanation read it, believe it, and hold firmly to it, for the holy Fathers' constant preoccupation was that they should unceasingly investigate the mystery of Holy Trinity, that they should believe what they discovered, and that they should hold these things as certain.

Many of those Fathers, looking upon the image of Holy Trinity as if in a mirror, confessed and adored it even before the coming of our Lord and Savior Jesus Christ.[2] One of them, for instance, when he sat beneath the elm of Mambre and saw three men walking down the road, is said to have understood these three as a figure of Holy Trinity, for he spoke to them as one.[3] "He saw three and adored one."[4] One in trinity and trinity in unity, that is Trinity.

Another of the Fathers, whose name I believe is not unknown to you, spoke thus in his poems, *May God, our God, bless us, may God bless us.*[5] When he says "God" the first time, he means the Father. When he says "God" again, he means the Son. When he says "God" a third time, he means the Holy Spirit. When he says of the Lord singularly, *and all the ends of the earth fear him,*[6] that author means that unity in trinity and trinity in unity must be believed to be true, confessed, and steadfastly adored.

15

Many others are said to have written extensively about this mystery. Paul, the famous preacher, says confidently about this Trinity, *For of him and in him and by him are all things.*[7] When Paul says *of him* he means the Father, *in him* the Son, and *by him* the Holy Spirit. When he says, *to him be glory,* in the same passage, he means threefold and singular power enduring without change. For those boys who were sent into the fiery furnace and there adored the image of Holy Trinity were found worthy to emerge unhurt.[8]

Therefore, my son, believe in the Father and the Son and the Holy Spirit with all your strength. How their divinity is coequal and their majesty coeternal! For as the Father is, so is the Son, and so also the Holy Spirit. Although they have different names in their respective persons, their threefold name—God, that is, Trinity, the Father and the Son and the Holy Spirit—nevertheless embraces them according to their nature.

Although it would be too lengthy a task to recount for you their individual attributes, I urge you that you believe in them, love them, and cherish them. Adhere to, believe in, and fulfill in action what you find in this book, the work of my small understanding. Then you may be saved from the fire of eternal damnation, and—along with the boys who were snatched from the fire[9]—you too may be found worthy to be united with the company of the elect in that kingdom without end. Amen.

2. On faith, hope, and charity.

Although three virtues are written about in books, one of them—that is, charity—is singular, the highest of them. "Hope," *spes,* is so called from "hoping for," *sperandum,* something that you have not yet attained but that you hope may come to be. Whatever you have already, you do not hope for, because you already feel the benefit of its possession. "Faith," *fides,* is so called from "believing," *fidendum.* You hope for something when you do not have it—a material object or a means of acquiring some benefit. Then, when you actually have attained it and possess it, you have faith in it because you now have the benefit of this thing that you used to hope for in your desire for it. Finally only the wish to keep it, that is, charity, remains. As the Apostle says, *faith, hope, and charity, these three: but the greatest of these is charity.*[10]

Earthly things teach what heavenly ones are, my son. When you struggle to acquire things on earth, you rejoice, as everyone does. But I urge you that your seeking and your finding be not only here, but also in the next world. Seek out diligently those things that are necessary for your soul. Ask for the former things, the earthly ones, but seek diligently for the latter ones. Say with the Psalmist, *O Lord . . . thou art my hope, my portion, in the land of the living.*[11] Believe in him, and good things will happen to you the more swiftly. *Trust in the Lord and do good. . . . be subject* to him and pray frequently. *Delight in him, and he will give thee the requests of thy heart.*[12] Keep your mind always on those things that are lofty and sublime, my son. If you do so, you will be found worthy to feed on those delights[13] because God, gentle and merciful, deigns to fill up all those who truly thirst and seek after him in all good things. Therefore believe, as I have said above, in the Father and in the Trinity. Ask for him in faith, seek diligently of him in hope, and beseech in charity that one who is called God.

Seek by thinking, ask by speaking, and beseech in your action that one from whom you hope to receive all good things. In these three activities, you will come to that highest and most perfect virtue, that is, charity. For "charity," *karitas*, is really a Greek word that in Latin means "love," *dilectio.*[14] Both these terms connote that highest being who is adored and worshiped, God. As Scripture says, *God is charity: and he that abideth in charity, abideth in God, and God in him.*[15] Love him, my son, and he will love you; cherish him, and he will cherish you. For he says, *I love them that love me: and they that in the morning early watch for me, shall find me.*[16] Again: *Behold, I stand at the gate, and knock. If any man* arise *and open to me this door, I will come in to him, and will sup with him, and he with me.*[17] *I will love him freely.*[18] Not only I, but *my Father will love him, and we will come to him, and will make our abode with him.*[19] May the Lord in his goodness bring your father to that feast and that mansion along with his children—and me as well. Amen.

3. *On reverence in prayer.*[20]

"Prayer," *oratio*, is so called from *oris ratio*, "the reason of the mouth."[21] And reverence is what we offer something worthy of respect, which we must seek out with the deep feeling of the heart and the clear force of reason.[22] If we seek of a man with great earthly power that he give us something useful, whether it be large or small, we seek this not with arrogance or loud protest or complaint, but we ask for it with all humility, so that he may command that what we seek be given. How much the more must we pray with respect to the founder and benefactor of all good things when we ask, seek, and find.[23] Not in a loud voice[24] nor in a lengthy speech but in deep and spontaneous feeling, in silence, we must seek of him that he give to us, endow us, enrich us, and deign to grant what we ask. In ancient times the holy Fathers prayed at great length and attained steadfast devotion in their pure petition. Why? Because in their great merits they were always with the Lord.

But I, Dhuoda—lukewarm and lax, fragile and always tending toward the depths—fail to take pleasure in short prayer, much less in long prayer. Still I have hope in him who permits the faithful to seek him. As for you, my son William, be vigilant. Seek him and pray to him in short, pure, direct speech. Offer your prayer not only in church but wherever circumstances take you. Pray and say: "Merciful one, you who take pity, and are just and good, forgiving and truthful, take pity on this being that you have made, whom you have created and redeemed with your blood. Take pity upon me.[25] Grant that I may walk in the pathways of your justice. Give me memory and intelligence so that I may understand you, believe in you, love, fear, praise, and give thanks to you, and reach the perfection of good deeds through righteous faith and good will, my Lord God. Amen."

Pray with your mouth, cry out with your heart, ask in your deeds that God come to your aid always, day and night, in every hour and every moment. As you lie quiet in your bed, say three times: *O God, come to my assistance. O Lord, make haste to help me,*[26] and then "gloria" up to the end. Then say the Lord's Prayer. When that is done, say: "Keep watch over me, Lord, throughout the day, and guard me in this night if such is your will. May you find me worthy to be protected *under the shadow of your wings,*[27] filled with the Holy Spirit, surrounded by your kingly defense, ringed by angel guardians, so that although I am restless in this night, I may sleep the sleep of peace. And if I wake in the night, may I feel that you are the guardian of my slumber, you the Savior who appeared on the ladder to the blessed Jacob."[28]

When you have done all this, make on your forehead and over your bed the sign of the cross of him by whom you were redeemed, in this fashion †,[29] and say at the same time: "I adore your cross, my Lord, and I believe in your holy resurrection. May your holy cross be with me. Your cross is the sign that I have always loved since I came to know it, and that I always adore. That cross is my salvation, my defense, my protection, and my constant refuge. That cross is my life[30] and your death, evil one, enemy of truth, lover of emptiness. That cross is my life, but it is death always to you." And again: "I adore your cross †, my Lord, and I contemplate your glorious passion—you who deigned to be born, to suffer, to die, and to rise again from the dead, you who are with the Father and the Holy Spirit †. May the blessing of God the Father and the Son and the Holy Spirit descend and remain upon me, the least of your servants. Amen."

May that cross and that benediction be always with those whom I in my weakness have often mentioned above.[31] *Like the dew of Hermon, which descendeth upon Mount Sion, like the precious ointment poured out* on the head, that ran down upon the beard, the beard of Aaron[32]—so may the unction of Jesus of Nazareth, the son of God, flow down upon you and remain with you wherever you may be. And may it remain with your brother, my second child, who came forth from my womb after you. Someday, if with God's help there are more among you,[33] may they too take heed of what I have asked above in the presence and help of him who lives and reigns always, through time without end. Amen.

Then when with God's help you get up in the morning, or at whatever hour the good Lord permits you so to do, say again three times, "O God, come to my assistance . . . ," as above, then the Lord's Prayer. When that is finished, say: "My king and my God, arise and help me.[34] Hear my cries, *for to thee will I pray: O Lord, in the morning thou shalt hear my voice.*[35] Rise up and take charge of my judgment, so that today you may plead my case, my God."

What more shall I say, my son? When you rise, put on your shoes as we always do and ready yourself *with the preparation of the gos-*

pel of peace.[36] Keep the canonical hours and fulfill your duty, as it is written: *Seven times a day I have given praise to thee.*[37] Throughout, say such scriptural verses as you know best or as occur to you. When you have done so, then say the proper prayers for the respective hours. Then go out in the name of the highest God to do the earthly service that awaits you, or whatever your lord and father Bernard or your lord Charles commands you to do, as God permits.

4. On the same topic.

When you go forth, keep God in your spirit with the sign of the cross and say: "Take pity on me, good father, and today *'perfect thou my goings in thy paths.'*[38] *Conduct me, O Lord, in thy way, and I will walk in thy truth.*[39] Come to my assistance, my God, today and always, so that insults may not befall me, nor any injustice overwhelm me. Make my heart joyful as I walk the good path, so that I may be found worthy in doing those things that are pleasing to you to reach the end of this day with your help." Then I will say: "*Blessed art thou, Lord God, because thou, . . . O Lord, hast helped me and hast comforted me.*[40] You are blessed, from whom all good things come, you who live" and so forth.

Book Three

1. *On the reverence you should show your father throughout your life.*
Now I must do my best to guide you in how you should fear, love, and
be faithful to your lord and father, Bernard, in all things, both when
you are with him and when you are apart from him. In this Solomon
is your teacher and your wisest authority. He chastises you, my son,
and says to you in warning, *For God hath made the father* who flourishes in his children *honorable.*[1] And likewise: *He that honoreth his
father shall have joy in his own children*[2] and *shall enjoy a long life.*
He that obeyeth the father shall be a comfort to his mother.[3] *As one
that layeth up* good things,[4] so is he who honors his father. *He that
feareth the Lord, honoreth his parents.*[5] So *honor thy father,* my son,
and pray for him devotedly, *that thou mayest be longlived upon the
land,*[6] with a full term of earthly existence. *Remember that thou hadst
not been born* but through him.[7] In every matter be obedient to your
father's interest and heed his judgment.[8] If by God's help you come to
this, *support the old age of thy father and grieve him not in his life.*[9]
Despise him not when thou art in thy strength.[10]

May you never do this last, and may the earth cover my body before
such a thing might happen. But I do not believe that it will. I mention
it not because I fear it but rather so that you may avoid it so completely
that such a crime never comes to your mind, as I have heard that it
indeed has done among many who are not like you.[11] Do not forget the
dangers that befell Elias's sons, who disobediently scorned the commands of their father and for this met with a bitter death.[12] Nor should
I fail to mention the tree[13] of Absalom, who rebelled against his father

and whom a base death brought to a sudden fall. Hung from an oak and pierced by lances, he ended his earthly life in the flower of his youth, with a groan of anguish. Lacking as he did an earthly kingdom, he never reached that highest of kingdoms promised to him.[14]

What of the many more who behave as he did? Their path is perilous. May those who perpetrate such evil suffer accordingly. It is not I who condemn them, but Scripture that promises their condemnation, threatening them terribly and saying, *Cursed is he that honoreth not his father.*[15] And again, *He who curseth his father, dying let him die*[16] basely and uselessly. If such is the punishment for harsh, evil words alone, what do you think will happen to those who inflict real injury upon their parents and insult the dignity of their fathers? We hear of many in our times who, thinking their present circumstances unjust, consider such crimes without taking into account the past. On them and on those like them fall hatred, jealousy, disaster, and calamity, and *nourishment to their envy.*[17] They lose rather than keep those goods of others that they seek, and they are scarcely able even to keep their own property. I say these things not because I have seen them happen, but because I have read about such matters in books. I have heard of them in the past, you hear about them yourself, and I am hearing them even now. Consider what will happen in the future to those who treat others in this fashion. But God has the power to bring even these people—if there are such—to lament their evil ways and, in their conversion, to do penance and be worthy of salvation. May anyone who behaves so ill stay away from you, and may God give him understanding.

Everyone, whoever he may be, should consider this, my son: if the time comes that God finds him worthy to give him children of his own, he will not wish them to be rebellious or proud or full of greed, but humble and quiet and full of obedience, so that he rejoices to see them. He who was a son before, small and obedient to his father, may then be fortunate in his own fatherhood. May he who thinks on these things in the hope that they will happen consider too what I have said above. Then "all his limbs" will work "in concert, peacefully."[18]

Hear me as I direct you, my son William, and "listen carefully," follow the "instructions . . . of a father."[19] Heed the words of the holy Fathers, and *bind them in thy heart*[20] by frequent reading so that *years of life may be multiplied to thee*[21] as you grow continually in goodness. For *they that wait upon*[22] God, blessing him, obeying the Fathers and complying freely with their precepts—such men *shall inherit the land.*[23] If you listen to what I say above and if you put it into worthy practice, not only will you have success here on this earth, but also you will be found worthy to possess with the saints what the Psalmist describes: *I believe to see the good things of the Lord in the land of the living.*[24] So that this other land may be your inheritance, my son, I pray that he who lives eternally may deign to prepare you to dwell there.

2. On the same topic, on reverence for your father.

In the human understanding of things, royal and imperial appearance and power seem preeminent in the world, and the custom of men is to account those men's actions and their names ahead of all others, as though these things were worthy of veneration and as though worldly power were the highest honor.[25] This attitude is testified in the words of him who said, *whether it be to the king as excelling, or to the governors.*[26] But despite all this, my wish is as follows, my son. In the smallness of my understanding—but also according to God's will— I caution you to render first to him whose son you are special, faithful, steadfast loyalty as long as you shall live. For it is a fixed and unchangeable truth that no one, unless his rank comes to him from his father, can have access to another person at the height of power.[27]

So I urge you again, most beloved son William, that first of all you love God as I have written above. Then love, fear, and cherish your father. Keep in mind that your worldly estate proceeds from his. Recognize that from the most ancient times, men who have loved their fathers and have been truthfully obedient to them have been found worthy to receive God's benediction from those fathers' hands.

3. On the examples of the early Fathers.

We read that Sem, the son of Noah, reached heaven because he loved his father, and so did his brother Japheth. Their father said over their heads as he blessed them: may God bless Sem and Japheth, and may he dwell in their tents;[28] may they prosper, may they flourish, and may they be enriched in all good things. What shall I say about Cham and others like him?[29] Is it not necessary for you to know? For it is very useful to discern the meaning of these examples. Let us think upon them always, turning toward those who have been good.

In obeying his father, Isaac was found worthy to share with his wife and descendants many goods in this world, for he received that father's benediction. Isaac is also called *laughter*[30] in holy Scripture, or "rejoicing," and "rejoicing" is a fitting name for one such as he, just as "mourning" is rightly applied to an idle, confused, and profligate man. So too Jacob, because he loved and obeyed his father, was found worthy to be snatched away from many tribulations and pressing difficulties. He received double and triple benediction from God and from his earthly father, and also from his mother and an angel. It was said to him, *I will bless thee, and I will multiply* your name *as the stars of heaven.*[31] You will be blessed and you will be called Israel,[32] *for if thou hast been strong against God, how much more shalt thou prevail against men?*[33]

Consider, my son, how strong those are in the secular world who are worthy of God's blessing because of their parents' merits and because of their own filial obedience. If such was the case for Jacob, then you too should fight, seek, struggle, and strive manfully in all situations that you too may be worthy to receive at least that blessing from him who is called God and to receive your inheritance along with Jacob. For it is according to Jacob's model that faults are washed away and vices overcome; all his enemies submitted to the weight of his gentleness as if they wore yokes in his service.[34] The creator of the world gave Jacob a wife, children, and much material wealth. We read of him that he was always satisfied and rich in this world and that he pleased God in every way.

And what shall I say of Joseph, Jacob's son, who was so loving and obedient to his father that he would have been willing to die for him if God and that father's merits had not protected him? Joseph was betrayed and accused because of his obedience to his father; he was sent to his brothers, and they sold him. But he feared and avoided fornication with women, maintaining chastity of the mind for God's sake and of the body for his earthly lord's sake. Thus he was worthy to be loved more than all the other servants of his lord. He was imprisoned, he was beaten, and he suffered greatly—all these things for his father's sake, and throughout he gave thanks to God. Finally he was set free of this swarm of troubles and hardships. He became the greatest of counselors and interpreters of dreams; he was raised to great authority and crowned with the highest power. In the royal hall, when he shone forth as the second in command on account of his merits, he was higher in rank than all the rest.

He was called *Joseph . . . a growing son, a growing son*,[35] and the Egyptians changed his name to ruler of the world and savior[36] because of the goodness of his great love. Beautiful in demeanor, beautiful in spirit, beautiful in appearance, he was still more beautiful in understanding, chaste in body and humble in heart. And what else shall I say? Eminent and rich in this world, he was pleasing in everything to God and man alike. Ruling his father and his brothers, governing all of Egypt, he ended his earthly life in peace. Walking *from virtue to virtue*,[37] he was found worthy in his humility, chastity, and obedience to be joined to God, shining forth in heaven and ruling with the saints in glory. And all this because of his devotion to his father.

Many others who have been obedient to God and mindful of the commands of a devoted father have been honored and respected in the secular world and have safely reached that heavenly reward for which they struggled. May what happened to them happen also for you if the good Lord grants you children. But what else shall I write for you about that humble respect I have described above? I beseech and I caution you that you act worthily toward deserving individuals.[38] Always do good works. And always grow and increase in him who is called God, the maker of heaven and earth, about whom it is written: and he was subject to his parents.[39] May the redeemer of the human race cause you to grow, to progress, and to be enlarged in age and wisdom before God and men.[40] May Jesus Christ, our Lord in whom all good things are possible and who reigns eternally, deign to grant these things to you. Amen.

4. *Direction on your comportment toward your lord.*
You have Charles[41] as your lord; you have him as lord because, as I believe, God and your father, Bernard, have chosen him for you to serve at the beginning of your career, in the flower of your youth. Remember that he comes from a great and noble lineage on both sides of his

family.[42] Serve him not only so that you please him in obvious ways, but also as one clearheaded in matters of both body and soul. Be steadfastly and completely loyal to him in all things.

Think on that excellent servant of the patriarch Abraham. He traveled a great distance to bring back a wife for his master's son.[43] Because of the confidence of him who gave the command and the wise trustworthiness of him who followed it, the task was fulfilled. The wife found great blessing and great riches in her many descendants. What shall I say of the attitude of Joab, of Abner, and of many others toward the king David?[44] Facing dangers on their king's behalf in many places, they desired with all their might to please their lord more than themselves. And what of those many others in holy Scripture who faithfully obeyed their lords' commands? Because of their watchful strength they were found worthy to flourish in this world. For we know that, as Scripture tells, all honor and authority are given by God. Therefore we should serve our lords faithfully, without ill will, without reluctance, and without sluggishness. As we read, *there is no power but from God: and he . . . that resisteth the power, resisteth the ordinance of God.*[45]

That is why, my son, I urge you to keep this loyalty as long as you live, in your body and in your mind. For the advancement that it brings you will be of great value both to you and to those who in turn serve you. May the madness of treachery never, not once, make you offer an angry insult. May it never give rise in your heart to the idea of being disloyal to your lord. There is harsh and shameful talk about men who act in this fashion. I do not think that such will befall you or those who fight alongside you because such an attitude has never shown itself among your ancestors. It has not been seen among them, it is not seen now, and it will not be seen in the future.[46]

Be truthful to your lord, my son William, child of their lineage. Be vigilant, energetic, and offer him ready assistance as I have said here. In every matter of importance to royal power take care to show yourself a man of good judgment—in your own thoughts and in public—to the extent that God gives you strength. Read the sayings and the lives of the holy Fathers who have gone before us. You will there discover how you may serve your lord and be faithful to him in all things. When you understand this, devote yourself to the faithful execution of your lord's commands. Look around as well and observe those who fight for him loyally and constantly. Learn from them how you may serve him. Then, informed by their example, with the help and support of God, you will easily reach the celestial goal I have mentioned above. And may your heavenly Lord God be generous and benevolent toward you. May he keep you safe, be your kind leader and your protector. May he deign to assist you in all your actions and be your constant defender. *As it shall be the will* of God *in heaven so be it done.*[47] Amen.

5. *On taking counsel.*[48]

If God should someday bring you to such a point that you are found worthy to be called to the council of the magnates, consider carefully on what, when, to whom, and how you should offer worthy and appropriate comment. Act with the advice of those who encourage you to behave loyally in body and in soul. It is written: do everything with counsel, *and thou shalt not repent when thou hast done.*[49] Here "everything" refers not to evil deeds offensive to good judgment, but to lofty and generous actions such as enhance the health of soul and body and are beyond reproach; such deeds are useful and steady, of long-enduring effect. As someone said, *what I have said is determined.*[50]

Those who do metalwork, when they begin to pound out gold to make it into leaf, wait for the best and most suitable day, weather, and temperature. Then the gold that they work for decoration, brilliant and sparkling even among the finest metals, may shine still more brightly.[51] In the same way, the thought of those in council should in all matters follow the well-reasoned pattern known to the wise. For the speech of one who has good understanding is whiter than snow, sweeter than honey, purer than gold or silver. Why? Because, as Scripture says, from the mouth of a wise man comes honey.[52] The eloquence of a great man is therefore a favor greater than silver and gold[53] because his lips draw from the honeycomb[54] and his words *are pure words . . . tried by the fire, purged.*[55]

There are no riches where stupidity reigns, and nothing is wanting, nothing an obstacle, in matters where gentle speech prevails.[56] Whoever tries to be numbered among the wise can be welcome to both God and man and pleasing in every way to his earthly lord. For he will be known as true as gold, seen as whiter than snow. It is written: the mouths of the wise will be bleached whiter than snow,[57] and their lips will be the lips of exaltation.[58] Such are the lips of those who, with thoughtful counsel, offer speech useful to both God and men and enduring in Christ after its good effect is accomplished.

As for you, my son, believe in God, fear him, and love him.[59] Do not hesitate to cling to him in the flower of your youth. Seek his wisdom and he will grant it to you. For the Apostle James says, *But if any of you want wisdom, let him ask of God, who giveth to all men abundantly, and upbraideth not,* but let him ask *nothing wavering, and it shall be given him,*[60] for God wishes to be petitioned. For the Lord says, encouraging us, *Ask, and it shall be given you: seek, and you shall find: knock, and it shall be opened to you.*[61] I believe confidently in that Lord's generous mercy, freely given. For he who beseeches the Lord with the worthy, pure love of the heart may ask to be given wisdom, counsel, and those other things necessary for the body. Such a man may then believe that God will open to him and that the Lord will give to him.[62]

Therefore, my son, pray and seek of the Lord, just as a certain man used to pray to him in song. Say with that poet: to you be praise, honor, and power. You who are rich in all things, *give me wisdom.* And again, *Give me wisdom, that sitteth by thy throne, and cast me not off from among thy children.*[63] Send *wisdom out from the throne of thy majesty, that she may be with me, and may labor with me,*[64] so that I may *discern between good and evil* and be able to judge which is better.[65] Love this wisdom, even from your youth, and seek it often as you invoke God. And if the good Lord should give it to you, cherish it, and it will embrace you in return. If you have wisdom, you will be the more blessed.

I urge you to make every effort to associate not only with older men who love God and seek wisdom but also with youths who do so, for maturity is rooted in the flower of youth. As someone says, *The things that thou hast not gathered in thy youth, how shalt thou find them in old age?*[66] So seek this in the Lord and say: God, teach me therefore from my youth, and unto old age and gray hairs[67] my good father will not desert me.[68] You will be blessed, my son, if you are made learned by him and if you are worthy to be instructed in his law. Indeed, Samuel and David were judges even as boys in the flower of youth according to

28

the custom of the Fathers, and they were again as old men.[69] They were great counselors to kings in the secular world, and they faithfully gave advice to the leaders of the Gentiles and foreign people. They deserved the victor's palm[70] because of their worthy merits.

Think on the Fathers who went before us; think about Joseph before Pharaoh,[71] Daniel before Nabuchodonosor, Baltassar, and Darius and the leaders of the Medes and the Persians.[72] Without abandoning their own ways, these Fathers were always helpful in council. Do not forget Jethro, Moses' kinsman, and how he gave important counsel,[73] or how Achior advised Holofernes, prince of the Gentiles,[74] or how many more of the ancients faithfully gave excellent counsel to their friends and those around them. In freeing themselves, they were found worthy both of spiritual salvation and of the bounty of those they counseled. Indeed, these Fathers shine forth in the sacred Scriptures, praised much more than others. Why? *Because God hath tried them, and found them worthy,*[75] humble and pure in mind and body, informed in their understanding, so that the Lord is known to have joined them, pure as gold, to himself. There is no doubt that they, like the sacrifice of the holocaust,[76] are brought together with him in his kingdom in spirit and in body along with all the saints.

What shall I, the unworthy, unlucky, and insignificant Dhuoda, say then of you, my son? I pray that he who strengthened those men and others like them, he who is called God, may also increase the strength of your manhood now and always. *Nevertheless as it shall be the will of God in heaven so be it done*[77] always in respect to you.

6. *More on the same topic. On counselors.*

There are some who consider themselves counselors and are not, for they think themselves wise even when this is untrue. *I speak as one less wise: I am more.*[78] But this is not the fault of him in whom all good flourishes. For there are those who give good counsel and do not do it in a good way but in a way neither useful to themselves nor uplifting to another. Why? Because the counsel of such men does not lead to the highest, perfect good of heaven. And there are many who give bad counsel, but without effect. This happens in many, various ways. There were in former times many worthy, good, and truthful men, but today most people are unlike those ancients in many ways.[79] What does this mean for us? Many things are clear in this secular world. For Scripture says, *and because iniquity hath abounded, the charity of many shall grow cold.*[80] As things are now, one does not know whom to choose as a counselor or whom one ought first to believe, and for many the hope of finding help from anyone remains uncertain. Read the *Synonyms.*[81]

But you must not despair in this, my son. There are many descended from these ancients who still, with God's help, are willing and able to give counsel that is good, welcome, and appropriate in respect to both themselves and their lords. And all these things happen through him who is called the Most High. For Scripture says, *Is there no physician in Egypt or balm in Galaad,*[82] clear water in Canaan or counselor in Israel? There is indeed, and clear understanding reveals itself in many men. God, who gives light to the world and is the angel of good counsel, knows his own. He shows them the words that bring the soul's salvation. May he who was then among the ancients and is now among the living, who is in you, goes out from you, and returns to you, who directs you to fight alongside a worthy, high king to carry out that earthly lord's command[83]—may that God cause you to arrive at that high, right counsel. Amen.

7. Special direction on the same topic.

For you to be such a man depends entirely on the judgment and the power of omnipotent God. If, with the aid of the highest creator, you come to the time that I have mentioned above,[84] fear immoral men and seek out worthy ones. Flee evil men and find good ones.[85] Do not take counsel with a man of ill will or a weak-spirited man or a wrathful man. For he will corrupt you like tin,[86] and under his command you will never rest secure. For the wrath and the envy that come easily to him draw him at once, headlong, to the depths.

Let not your fate be like Achitofel's[87] or like Aman's,[88] bad and arrogant men whose counsels were worthless and who, when they gave bad advice to their lord, fell headlong in both spirit and body to their deaths. For I wish, my son, that you take pleasure in fighting on your lord's behalf, as did such men as Doeg the Edomite[89] and the humble Mardochai.[90] Achitofel offered Absalom the bad counsel that

30

he should rebel against his father, David—and Achitophel did so in order to win the son's favor. But by the will of God,[91] Achitophel's evil counsels were brought to nothing.[92] But Chusai[93] and Doeg, a strong man who firmly held his ground against another determined man,[94] remained unshakable in their counsel. On the other hand Aman, on account of the pride in his envious spirit, gave evil counsel to Assuerus so that sons of Israel were killed.[95] But Mardochai, praying for God's help to liberate himself and his people, gave the same king good counsel, the evidence of loyalty, in order to free and to vindicate himself.[96] Mardochai began, "Consider, O king."[97]

By God's providence, one man merits salvation with his people. Another, a proud man, goes away empty along with all his house. He is hung on the gallows that in his envy he has prepared for the humble man, so that this evil is turned upon its designer. All by himself he has brought his life, even his body, to a worse end. There is fulfilled in him and in those like him what is said: *He hath conceived sorrow, and brought forth iniquity. He hath opened a pit . . . and fallen into it.*[98] For he who had prepared evil for his innocent brother has now rushed headlong and straightaway into death. God, who is good and who in his goodness spares the wicked, rightly desires to bring all men to himself through penance. For *he knoweth both the deceiver, and him that is deceived* by the deceiver.[99]

Therefore, my son William, fear immoral men and seek out worthy ones. Flee evil men like those mentioned here, but attach yourself to good men seeking after worthy goals. They offer counsel in the most useful of ways, in their true subjection to the wishes of their lords, and they are found worthy to receive fitting reward both from God and in the secular world.[100] I pray that such counsel as has been in those great men may grow in you now, every day, always, my best of sons.

8. *Regarding your lord's family.*

As for the great and famous relations and associates of your royal lord —those who are descended from his illustrious father's side as well as those related to him by marriage[101]—fear, love, honor, and cherish them if you and those who fight alongside you are found worthy to serve them in the royal and imperial court or anywhere else you may act on their behalf. In all undertakings in their interest maintain a pure, fitting, and steadfast obedience to them, as well as good faith in the execution of your duties.

Remember how David comported himself toward Jonathan, the son of the king Saul. In every way, throughout his life, he was a pure, faithful, and true supporter of both the father and the son, and also their children, not only during their lives but also after their deaths. Even after their destruction the sweetness of his great love caused him to mourn them with sorrowful tears, greatly lamenting and saying, *How are the valiant fallen in battle*[102] and *the weapons of war perished?*[103] And also, *I grieve for thee, my brother Jonathan: exceedingly beautiful, and amiable to me above the love of women,*[104] *swifter than eagles, stronger than lions.*[105] And again, my best of children, *the arrow of Jonathan never turned back.*[106] In these and other instances David was filled with grief for the king's son, and with his retainers he mourned deeply over Jonathan's ruin. May you and those who fight alongside you avoid such a fate.

I am having this copied out as an example for you.[107] For when David recovered, as if consoled by the great loyalty of his love for them, he praised his dead friends in another voice, with sighing, *Saul and Jonathan, lovely, and comely in their life, even in death they were not divided.*[108] Many who faithfully obeyed the commandments of their lords and their lords' relations are abundantly and honorably praised in sacred Scriptures. Read the book of Kings and the books of the other Fathers, and you will find many.

So, my son William, bear patiently the yoke that governs a servant and be faithful to your lord Charles—whatever sort of lord he may be[109]—and to his worthy relations of both sexes and to all those of royal origins. It is fitting for you and for all those who fight under their royal power to do so, and I wish that you serve them to good ends, faithfully, with all your might. For as we believe, God chose them and established them in royal power, granting them glory almost as great in its likeness to the ancients' as that promised to Abraham, Isaac, and Jacob,[110] and to their worthy children and descendants.

May the omnipotent Father—our strong King, the glorious Highest—make them peaceful and harmonious, seeking concord after the manner of their fathers in this earthly realm.[111] Then they may shine in prosperity and rule, protect, and govern the world and its people with strength in the service of God and his saints.[112] And they may hold and defend our people from the blows of enemies pressing all around, uniting the holy church of God the more firmly in Christ and his true religion. May they see the children of their sons pleasing God in worthy fashion, growing and flourishing, and aiming for heaven through many cycles of the years, persevering in this course until they come happily to the end of their lives. As for you, after you have reached the end of this present life, may he who gives all recompense and all bounty bring you to rest in the kingdom of heaven with those Fathers whom I have mentioned. May he bring you to his kingdom and his glory—you who struggle here to render faithful service both to your several earthly lords and to that singular Lord who gives fitting reward for your merits from his own riches. And may he unite you happily to Christ.

9. *Regarding the magnates.*

As for the magnates and their counselors—and all those like them who serve faithfully—show them your love, affection, and service often. Do so to them together and individually, to whomever is important at court. Learn attentively from the model of their distinction and adhere to it firmly. For in a house as great as the king's there are, there have been, and there will be, if the good Lord so commands, many conversations. There, one who wishes can learn from others humility, charity, chastity, patience, gentleness, modesty, sobriety, discretion, and other virtues, as well as the desire to do good.

So, my son, while you are a young boy still growing,[113] learn from those elders whose understanding is rich whatever good you can with the Father's help so you may be pleasing to God before all else and then be useful to man. I urge you to strive to act among your associates, peers, and faithful friends so that your life may hold to a good course, marked with no shame of disloyalty to your lords but with eagerness for good action, in a laudable fashion, worthy and proper. May that God who makes the tongues of infants speak in his praise— as it is written, *out of the mouths of infants*[114]—himself cause you, filled with the eloquence of worthy, noble men who fear the Lord, to climb to the ranks of heaven.

10. *That you accommodate yourself to great and to lesser men.*

I need not point out to you that great men as well as lesser should follow the examples of their lords and of the highest magnates. Far from me as you are, you realize that constantly yourself. Still, never doubt that even lesser folk improve themselves after the model of their betters. I urge you not to hesitate to attach yourself to them—and them to you—by large and small favors.

God is the maker of all good things in heaven and earth, but he deigned to show his presence even here below for the sake of the least of his creatures. For as the learned say, even though he is the Most High and the creator of all things, he deigned to take on the form of a servant.[115] He raises up the powerful so that they may be cast down to the depths, and he exalts the humble[116] in order then to raise them up to a higher state. It is he, as the prophet says, who is the littlest one multiplying to a thousand, the weak one who becomes the strongest nation.[117] He is great among the least of men, the feeble; he is powerful and manly. We believe in one God, creator, shepherd, and governor of our bodies and our souls, namely that one about whom I have written above. We receive all things from him, whatever seems to be within our power. Every higher creature with the faculty of reason should undoubtedly, whether he is greater or lesser than another, serve and praise his maker; such is fitting. And according to the authority of Scripture, the earth with all that is born of her, *the old with the younger*,[118] should bless God and give him praise.

There is a short saying: *Let every spirit praise the Lord.*[119] For it is he who loves the human race, and he does not fail to enrich through his gifts both the great and the small, according to his measure and on the scale of their merits. For he is *not a respecter of persons*, but in all things, when he is besought, he is present to those who fear him[120] and who do his will.

And if he who is so great acts thus even toward the least of men, what should we who are ourselves of small importance do for those who are even lesser? Those who can give aid should do so and—according to the words and injunctions of the Apostle—carry burdens for each other,[121] the strong for the weak, the capable for those who are not. Then the weak may climb along with the strong, participating in their strength, to that heavenly height promised our forefathers. For the same Apostle says: Now you *that are stronger* and more powerful *ought to bear the infirmities of the weak,*[122] so that your *abundance may supply their want*[123] and their poverty.

My son, although you may be the least in stature among those who fight alongside you, you are nevertheless steadfast in your mind. Do not hesitate, I therefore urge you, to examine closely and to imitate the exemplary strength and model of those great men of whom you have read above. Consider great men as high above you, your equals as your betters, and those like you as ahead of you, so that in your attachment to them you may advance the dignity of your ancestors. Rejoice in deep humility, I beseech you, that they all have been set before you as your examples.

For instance, consider the image, metaphorically expressed, of the man about whom it is written, *his hand will be against all men, and all men's hands against him.*[124] If we understand this short description in a good sense, then I urge that you be such a man in all respects. Then your hand will be ready for worthy action, and you will do your best now and always to give service and honor—not only in words but in deeds, and with gentle speech—to great men, to lesser men, to those who are your equals, and likewise to the least of men. For it is written about our obligation to give, *God loveth a cheerful giver.*[125] And it is said about words that a good speech is better than the *best gift.*[126] So you must do both things. If you strive to apply yourself with good will toward all, there will be accomplished in you what is written above. And may your hand, giving free service, be against all in order to give, and may all hands be against you to help you or to reward you according to the merit of your actions.

Love all so that you may be loved by all, and cherish them that you may be cherished. If you love all, all will love you.[127] If you—who are singular—love them, then they—who are plural—will love you. It is written in Donatus's *Art of Poetry,* "I love you and I am loved by you, I kiss you and am kissed by you, I cherish you and am cherished by you, I respect and am respected by you." And again, "I, of me or by me, of me or from me, and O, by me" and more of the same, "them, of them or by them, O, by them," and many other relevant things.[128]

Therefore, my son William, cherish and show respect to whatever one or many persons you wish to respect you. Love, revere, stand by, and honor all, so that you may be found worthy to receive appropriately honorable recompense in all the changeable situations of the world. Toward our edification in this regard a certain learned author offers a brief comparison—an important one, extraordinarily clear in its meaning—with dumb animals. He says in the forty-first Psalm, *As the hart panteth.* For this is what harts do when groups of them begin to cross seas or wide streams with churning waves—they lower their necks one after the other, each putting his head and horns on the back of the previous one, so that as they each rest a little they all may the more easily cross the swift current. The harts have such intelligence and such commensurate discretion that, when they perceive that the one in front is weakening, the leader becomes a follower and eventually the last in line so that the others may assist and support him; then they choose another to go first. Thus, as one individual takes the place of another, each feels the brotherly fellowship of love run through them all. Always careful that the head and antlers of any one of their kind not be plunged into the flood, the harts manage to hold up his head [129] and to keep his antlers visible.

The point of this is not obscure to the learned, for everything is immediately clear in their sight. In the harts' mutual support—in their changing places in line—they show that human beings too must have the brotherly fellowship of love for greater and lesser men alike, in all ways and in all circumstances. We read that this was fulfilled in the past by many men, especially among the holy apostles and those like them. It is written, *For neither was there any one needy among them,*[130] *but all things were common unto them.*[131] They had *one heart and one soul* [132] in God, always feeling brotherly compassion for each other in Jesus Christ.

Just as the harts support and sustain each other's heads and antlers, so those who have faith in Christ hold up their hearts and keep their minds always on him. He who was born king of David's seed for the salvation of the human race and descended to the depth of this sea of battering waves has raised his horn to liberate his people.[133] Acting of his grace, he has found those who were lying in darkness, and rising from that depth he has visited them [134] and raised them to the heights. He offers his example lest we be lost in the turmoil of the deep sea or in the blinding mud of desire and cupidity, so that we may hold up our hearts in perseverance and say with the Apostle, *But our conversation is in heaven.*[135]

What of the lions and boars and other sensate animals? And what of the vine clinging to the earth or the elm reaching toward the sky, that edify us in their turn? There are many useful examples available to men. Read what is said in the appropriate books, and you will find out. *Speak to the earth, and it shall answer thee*, it is written, and *ask . . . the beasts, and they shall teach thee; and the birds of the air, and they shall tell thee . . . and the fishes of the sea shall tell.*[136] The meaning of this passage is indeed useful, and it is clear to some who know it. For there is one Creator and Restorer. He has seen fit to choose man before all the other beings to be in charge of them, according to a certain poet. As he says in his verses:

A virgin, he created the earth; a virgin, he created a virgin man,
And he was later made man of another virgin.
Alas, oh grief! The virgin man was corrupted—
Oh grief, alas!—the virgin woman was corrupted,
Yielding, both of them, to the serpent.[137]

Likewise the same poet:

On that account he will leave his father and mother,
And will cleave to his wife.
The two will be one flesh,
Commanding all that is subject to them,
Raising their estate by the use of reason.[138]

And again:

He who gave to man all the things
That heaven and earth and sea generate
In sky and stream and field—
Whatever the eye can see or hand feel—
This he set under their sway, and they under his.[139]

The meaning of this, my son William, is that the Highest, the omnipotent one, saw fit that man be fashioned out of the mud of the earth to replenish the number of his angels and to be joined to their high rank.[140] Granting to man the use of all things, God chose him to enjoy the great glory of eternity in his Lord's company. For man God willed that he be born, suffer, rise again, ascend to heaven, so that according to the measure of their goodness [141] he might join great and lesser men to himself and bring them to his heavenly kingdom.

What more could I or might I say to you by way of example of those who are of differing status—subjects or equals or even those of low estate—but joined together by love? With God's help, you know this already, and you will always be able to learn more concerning the standard of him who made all life. Great and greatly to be praised,[142] granting his bounty to the mighty and the small, may he cause you and all those mentioned above, as well as those who like them adhere to Christ, to be joined to him. And then may you come to that Lord who holds the mighty in his embrace and gathers in the small, praising them in saying, *Suffer the little children to come unto me . . . for of such is the kingdom* of heaven.[143] And may this happen with the help and grace of him who reigns without end in heaven. Amen.

11. *On respect for priests.*[144]

Priests are to be revered, my son, because they have been chosen for God's ministry and because, in holding sacred orders, they intercede for our sins. So fear God and honor his priests with all your soul. Love them and revere them. It is they who bless the chrism and the oil. It is they who baptize the people in the faith of Holy Trinity, uniting them with the holy church of God. It is they who consecrate the bread and the wine in the likeness of the body and blood of our Lord Jesus Christ, preparing the table and giving us communion *unto remission of sins* [145] and for the health of the body.

They are called *sacerdotes*, "priests," in order to sanctify or consecrate them after the example of him who said, *Be holy because I am holy.*[146] And again, *Follow peace with all men, and holiness: without which . . .* [147] and so forth. They are called priests, for the Prophet says, *You shall be called the priests of the Lord* our God.[148] They will wear down the Gentiles' strength, and *they shall eat the sins of my people.*[149] They are the shepherds who do not fail to feed the flock of the Lord through words and examples and who invite the people to the kingdom of God so that they do not hesitate to enter, but say with the Psalmist: *Come let us adore and fall down: and weep before the Lord that made us. For he is the Lord our God: and we are the people* and the sheep *of his pasture.*[150]

Priests are also called *presbyteri* for the reason that they are ready and prepared for the work of God; for in this word we use *prae* for *ante*, "before," as the Psalmist says: I have seen the Lord before,[151] that is through the contemplation of the mind I have seen him in advance. We mean something similar when we say "precursor," that is, one who goes before and precedes, or takes his place before.[152] Thus it is the priests among us who—on account of their worthy merits— approach the altar, warning us to have a ready heart[153] and that *our conversation is in heaven.*[154] They are the path through the example of whose preaching we travel confidently toward our heavenly fatherland through the practice of good works.

Bishops are called *episcopi* and "overseers"[155] because they admonish us always to be alert in our direction and goal. For *epi* in Greek is *super*, "over," in Latin. *Scopon* in Greek, in the same fashion, is *intuitio* or *destinatio*, "sight" or "objective," in Latin.[156] And so it is the responsibility of bishops to reveal each man to others, and our responsibility to observe and to obey those bishops. For priests are also called *pontifices* because we cross to our fatherland through them as on a *pons*, a "bridge," across a river.[157] That is, we cross and do not tarry in the malice of the heart as in churning mud. We are corrected through penance and amends, and with God's help we touch upon no foreign shore. It is written, *they went back another way into their country.*[158]

Bishops, after the model of the true and sublime Lord, are the bearers of authority above, below, within, and outside. They have authority above for the reason that they give protection by looking out afar, as they take up a point of observation at a distance. For through their learning and by the example of their chastisement, the Lord gathers us together from far-off lands. And bishops have authority below because they are the feet that bring peace, announce good tidings, preach salvation, and speak to Sion.[159] They have authority within because we are imbued with the example of their worth and wisdom; we are made learned and satisfied by them. And they have authority outside because through their constant prayer, staying as they do close to God, we are found worthy to be surrounded, fortified, protected, and kept safe, so that evil spirits do not seize us. Only thus we are able to direct ourselves toward him who appeared in the world and who was made our salvation and our support, so that he might recall fallen man to the heavenly fatherland.

And what may I say of those who are so worthy of reverence? My spirit shrinks from this task. It is priests who, according to the example of the holy apostles, bind and loose,[160] and they *eat the sins of the people.*[161] They are closer and nearer to God. They are the fishermen and the hunters, as the Prophet says, *Behold I will send* my *fishers . . . and they shall fish them: and . . . I will send* my *hunters, and they shall hunt them.*[162] They seize the prize from the hands of others, that is from unclean spirits, and by penance they join those they have captured to the company of their heavenly fatherland. These priests fashion and assemble the holy altar to stand in its proper place. For Scripture says: and the priests and Levites brought in the altar of the Lord into its place, *into the holy of holies under the wings of the cherubim.*[163] For such are the properties of priests' titles. Although the names applied to them vary according to their rank and activity, still they are properly called priests or keepers of vessels, that is, of the souls that belong to God. For what better can we call the ranks of the priesthood than the company to be joined with the ranks of the angels and of the citizens of heaven? For they are called angels, as the prophet Zacharias says, *the lips of the priest . . . keep knowledge, and* the people *seek the law at his mouth: because he is the angel of the Lord*, and not just an angel but the angel *of hosts.*[164]

What can be more sublime than the angels and archangels? Because of their merits they are so agile as to reach the sacred windows in their flight[165] as do the watchful doves. Glorying in their worthy virtues, deservedly—in a fashion that is clear to understand—they are called the friends of God. Why? Because they are filled with the fervor of charity. Their living example never ceases to inform the many. As Scripture says, they are clothed in justice,[166] joined with the company of the saints. Joyful and holy and flourishing in Christ, they are found worthy, with the acquisition of a double treasure, to reach the sublime kingdom of heaven.

Since priests have so many and such great names and virtues that their dignity in the secular world is so brilliant, I urge you to render them, worthy as they are, as much honor as you can. As for those whose personal merit is not adequate to their sacred office—even if you realize this about them—do not hastily judge them but shrink from condemning their way of life, as many do. Think on David. When he cut the border of Saul's cloak he was sorry.[167] And so we should not condemn priests, my son. God knows their hearts and the hearts of all who struggle in the secular world. Their fruit and their achievement are known to be worthy from their appearance, their speech, their understanding, and their life. As it is written, *by their fruits you shall know them.*[168]

What more shall I say? The Lord knows his own.[169] Still, take as your models those priests whom you find to be the better among them, more clearheaded in word and deed. Such men, even more than others, announce to us the word of God; they are the people chosen for his holy inheritance.[170] Listen to what they say, consider it, accomplish it, and think back upon it often. Wherever you encounter such priests, act humbly toward them and revere them—not only them but also the angels who go before them. For as sacred Scripture says, their angels always see the face of the Father.[171] May you dine often, if you can, with them and with hungry pilgrims. As I have said above, do not hesitate to entrust yourself into the hands of honorable priests. Find in them, among all those loyal to you, counselors when you have need. Listen to those who you see are especially close to God. Let them give food and drink to the poor from your hand and your table, and you will receive your reward in the aftermath.

So, my son William, as I have already said, revere those worthy priests who are God's servants. They are the chosen of God, and they are his helpers and his worshipers. If their behavior is not as it should be, do not—as is written—revile them. The sacred Scripture says in part of them: *touch ye not my anointed,* that is, those touched by my chrism; *do not evil to my prophets,*[172] that is, my priests. For in the house of the Lord *there are many mansions,*[173] and the stars of heaven do not gleam so brightly. For *star differeth from star in glory,*[174] and the just are brighter than the others because of the variety of their merits. In the same way there are differences among priests. Some *instruct many* through the example of their good works, drawing laymen along with them to Christ *as stars for all eternity,*[175] as we believe. And this is God's gift. But revere them, my son, as I have said, and if you are remiss in something, correct it. *For there is no man who sinneth not*[176] even if his life is as short as a single day.[177] But there is only one creator, shaper, ruler, and governor. On account of God and as his gift, the Lord's words come forth from the priest, for he grants this to us not according to our sins but according to his ancient mercy. In offering us this release, the Lord is called good, gentle, and merciful; he is, he has been, he will always be. May you know that it is he in whom, always and everywhere, true and learned priests find their understanding.

Offer them your true confession as best you know how—in privacy, with sighing and with tears. As the learned authors say, true confession liberates the soul from death[178] and prevents it from going to hell. Do not hesitate, I urge you, to entrust your mind and body to the hands of priests. When you are busy or at rest, or whatever you do or is done to you, always ask and pray that they deign to pray for you, interceding with that God who chose them as his people's intercessors in this world. Then you may deserve to be found worthy, as you devote half your days to penance[179] through true amends and worthy reparation, to be granted what he has promised to his saints.

May that true priest who is pontifex for eternity[180] bring you to true and worthy progress as you study and struggle in earthly service and as you follow the good examples of the ministers of his holy church. Through the help and grace of that God who reigns through all time, amen.

Book Four

1. *Special direction on various aspects of moral betterment.*
Among the human race, to attain perfection requires the application
of great and constant effort. We must apply to various evils the reme-
dies that are their antidotes.[1] We not only must overcome the influence of those worldly people who burn in the jaws of envy, but also—
as the Apostle says—we must overcome *the spirits of wickedness in
the high places.*[2] For there are some people who are successful in this
world and rich in material things but who still, out of some hidden
malice, constantly envy and tear away at others as much as they can,
all the while pretending to be of good will.

As the *Synonyms* say, "hidden evil is decorated with sweet words."[3]
It begins in men's hearts at the instigation of the devil, author of death.
We find it written, *The tabernacles of robbers abound, and they provoke God boldly.*[4] What is to the advantage of one is to the ruin of
another, so the text says also, *Anger killeth* the young man, *and envy
slayeth the little one.*[5] May you never act in this way, my son. No one
would be envious if he were not small in spirit in the first place, for
he who is small is he who lacks great things. Why is it that a man so
yearns for high rank that, driven by the spurs of envy, he loses himself
in body and in spirit? But this was what happened in the beginning,
as is written, *By the envy of the devil, death came into the world.*[6]
The same plague, befalling people each day, still tears many of them
to pieces. That twisting, many-shaped serpent-demon[7] never ceases to
penetrate the homes and to overturn the temples of those who try to
stand firmly in the faith of Christ. Always he *goeth about seeking* men

43

and women *whom he may devour.*[8] According to the verses of a certain learned author, his throng never ceases by day or night to take away from the faithful of the holy church of God the sign[9] that that devil knows endures to his destruction. For the poet says:

> Always grinding his teeth, chained in his dark cavern,
> He is out of his mind, driven by savage rage,
> He plunges himself and his maddened company in the black waves.[10]

The meaning of this is clear to men of learning: that devil is everywhere. He is this man and he is those men, if they are more than one—and I warn you, beware, flee, avoid them. Strive to distance yourself from their company. Put them behind your back, I urge you, and be quick to oppose them.

You already have books—and you will have them—in which to read, ponder, contemplate, study, and understand. And you also have learned men who may teach you, by whose example you may easily discover what is good in both aspects of your duty.[11] So it is that doves, even while they drink from clear fountains, watch for predatory herons and falcons, so that they are not caught. Flying away with laughter, they escape to where their pleasure takes them.[12] You too will do so if you seek out in your reading the words of the orthodox saints and of those Fathers who have gone before us. And you will do so if you observe frequently how the greatest of the magnates and counselors, as I have said above, fulfill the commands of God and of their earthly lords with faithful assent. If you follow their example with unfailing watchfulness, you will be able to escape not only from the unseen snares of evil spirits, but also from those visible enemies who stretch out their claws in this world. You will then be able easily to rise up in spiritual and physical strength and to reach your goal with Christ's help. Read and consider carefully the words of Solomon: *Let us now praise men of renown.*[13]

Although we are unimportant exiles,[14] and although we are not among the number of the great—because we carry in us the faults of this world and are always pulled downward rather than lifted toward heaven—nevertheless we are taught according to the admonition of the Old Testament to bear the twelve patriarchs' names written on our foreheads.[15] In the same way, according to the vision of Ezechiel, holy Scripture commands us to take as our examples those creatures who have six wings and eyes in front and back.[16]

Still I offer you this as a guiding principle—that you detest and flee the wicked, the immoral, the sluggish, and the proud and that in all you do you avoid those who are abhorrent in spirit. Why? Because they cast out strings, like mousetraps, in order to deceive. They never cease to prepare a road to scandal and offense, so that they themselves fall down recklessly and make others like them tumble with them. This has happened in the past, and I urge you that you avoid it now and in the future. May God forbid that your fate be linked in any way with theirs.

Seek out, hold close, and observe faithfully the examples of great men in the past, present, and future—men who are known to be pleasing in their faith to both God and this world, men who have persevered. For that is the meaning of the Scripture that commands us to hold the written names of the twelve patriarchs in our hands and to wear them on our foreheads, and to keep our eyes looking backward and forward;[17] this Scripture concerns virtue. While the men it describes were in this present world, they were always headed toward heaven, growing and flourishing toward God. Wise in faith and spirit, happy in their path,[18] they undertook and accomplished worthy ends through thought and deed. Then they left behind for us an example, so that in seeking it, we may do as they did.

2. *On the same topic.*

But you, my son, while you fight in this secular world[19] among all the earth's confusion, whatever good or bad things should befall you—I urge you to give thanks to God in all of them without ceasing. You should do so, however, always in this spirit: that in good times your mind should never be puffed up after the example of evil men, and that in bad times you never lose yourself or be cast down.

If ever faults should assail you, which I hope is not the case, set opposites against opposites, as I have said above. The Apostle says: *Walk in the spirit, and you shall not fulfill the lusts of the flesh. For the flesh lusteth against the spirit, and the spirit against the flesh.*[20] The Fathers of past times successfully fought this desire in themselves in a spirit of gentleness and forgiveness. As is written, while they grew in virtues and wrought justice, they were found worthy to conquer kingdoms through their faith.[21] *Unto old age and grey hairs*[22] they kept the covenant of God[23] and fulfilled his commandments. So these Fathers were found worthy to be exalted in this world, rejoicing in their sons and in their earthly possessions. Afterward too they had thrones prepared for them in heaven[24] by that Lord whom they loved in spirit and body, so that they might find rest. You know that this was true for all of them. For there is fulfilled in such men, in the way that they behaved, the poem offered by the Psalmist, *They shall go from virtue to virtue: the God of gods shall be seen in Sion.*[25]

There is strife today among many men. I even fear that it will extend to you and those who fight alongside you, for, as the Apostle says, *The days are evil.*[26] Again: *For there shall arise false* Christs,[27] and there *shall come dangerous times. Men shall be lovers of themselves, covetous, haughty, proud, blasphemers, disobedient to parents . . . lovers of pleasures more than of God.*[28] And this would be too long to describe in individual instances—alas—because already we see such men rising up in many ranks as if they see themselves on the point of victory.

So rouse yourself and pray, as I have said above, and say with the Psalmist: *Judge thou, O Lord, them that wrong me: overthrow them that fight against me. Take hold of arms and shield: and rise up to help me,*[29] *Lord, the strength of my salvation,*[30] *deliver me from them that surround me.*[31] *Say to my soul, do not fear, I am thy salvation.*[32] For there was one who asked in this fashion, and the answer came back to him, *Fear not . . . I am thy protector, and thy reward exceeding great.*[33] Each man who seeks the author of his salvation with his whole heart should believe that he can attain the salvation not only of his body but of his soul. As you ponder this over and over, make haste now and in the future to be so watchful in the struggle that you are confident of your salvation in both regards through that Lord whom you ought to have clearly in your sight.

3. *On the same topic. Useful direction.*

If pride[34] should at some point swell up in you—may this not befall!—keep in mind, lest it ever take charge of your heart, that God *resists the proud*[35] and casts them down to the depths. Fear pride and flee it, and apply profound, honest humility in all situations to cure this sickness of plague-ridden mortality. The humble, truthful maker of the human race gives his grace to the humble. For he says, *learn of me, because I am meek, and humble of heart.*[36]

O, how dire is this disease, the plague of pride. Because of it Lucifer, the great creature whom a great creator deigned to make, fell down into murky darkness and then further, headlong, into the depths. He rushed down into the craw of death's agonies, and he and all his following were delivered into endless hell.[37] But O how sublime and how heavenly is humility, for the humble Lord comes down with it from that same place whence the evil one, evilly self-deluded, was cast down through pride. Then the Lord causes those who share his humility to climb up step by step to find peace in heaven.[38] In that place there is the rest and peace of him who said: on whom shall I rest? on him that is humble and quiet and that *trembleth at my word?*[39]

4. *On arming yourself with the sevenfold gifts of the Holy Spirit.*[40]

If you are humble and peaceful, my son, you will surely be able to receive, at least in part, the seven gifts of the grace of the Holy Spirit from him whom I often mention above. Then the good spirit of the Lord will rest upon you. In being humble and obedient, you will easily be able to exchange the yoke of evil spirits for the yoke of Christ. As he says, *For my yoke is sweet and my burden light.*[41] Indeed, that man who bears the yoke and the burden of Christ is himself borne from the depths to highest heaven. The blessed apostle Peter said, when he ended his happy course in glorious suffering, "God, my master, raised to heaven on a tall cross, has also seen fit to transfer me from earth to heaven."[42]

Therefore, my son, learn in the strength of your youth to carry the yoke and the burden of Christ your king each day, in both spirit and body. Then, freed from the heavy burden of the shackles of sin, you will be secure and peaceful. You will be able to climb up and reach the Lord easily, with a light step, at least at the end of your life. As a certain learned author says in his sermon for the Friday of our Lord's passion,[43] each of us should choose conversion to God among all the uncertainties of this world, so that he may in the end be set free. The Psalmist says: Lord, *have regard to thy covenant,*[44] and *forget not to the end the souls of thy poor.*[45] Here, I think, "end" means the end of this life. So I urge you constantly, lest you perish, to take careful consideration of that end. And I wish that you may act as you serve on earth among your fellow soldiers so that in the end you may be found worthy to be included as a free soul among the free, with the servants and soldiers of Christ who serve together and not alone, in that kingdom without end.

If you struggle watchfully in this way, as I have said above, not only will you be found worthy to be endowed with the sevenfold infusion of the gifts of the Holy Spirit's grace, but you will be able in the end, in contemplating good works, to reach the high rank of the eight beatitudes.[46] I wish that you may always flourish in these virtues and these gifts.

It is said about the two kinds of resources for those who struggle in this world, *Give a portion to seven, and also to eight.*[47] For there are seven gifts of the Holy Spirit, as the prophet Isaias writes, *the spirit of wisdom, and of understanding, the spirit of counsel, and of fortitude, the spirit of knowledge, and of godliness . . . and the spirit of the fear of the Lord.*[48] But in another sense there are three kinds of spirits, that is the spirits of angels, of men, and of animals or reptiles.[49] Still, the gifts of the Holy Spirit are numbered seven for good reason—that there are seven days of the week, seven ages of the world, and seven lamps that light the holy of holies.[50]

If you love God with your whole heart and study carefully the volumes of his scriptures in the Old and New Testaments, and if you do this reading with appropriate concentration, then the spirit of wisdom will come to rest upon you. For *all wisdom is from the Lord God,*[51] nor can it be otherwise because *it hath been always with him, and is before all time.*[52] If you study such wisdom carefully and accept it firmly, you will be blessed and you will be able to be called wise. The Lord will conduct you in a wondrous path[53] as he directs and protects you with his holy right hand, leading you to eternal and bountiful life and enfolding you in his embrace. Then the spirit of wisdom will rest upon you.

If you carefully consider the words of our Lord, as Osee says: search out his ways.[54] And again, *then shall you know that I am he.*[55] If you understand that threats of eternal punishment and hell are reserved to sinners and that worthy deeds are rewarded with the glory of reign among the worthy,[56] there will rest upon you the spirit of understanding. The Psalmist asked for this spirit when he said, *Give me understanding, and I will search thy law; and I will keep it with my whole heart.*[57] Hide it away in your heart so that you may persevere in it. If you do this, you will have as your companion the spirit of understanding.

If in good fortune and in bad you walk the straight path—and at the same time with such an attitude that you are not downcast in adversity or lightheaded in prosperity, but seek the Lord's counsel—so that in both aspects of your activity you are found worthy of the Lord's assistance, then the spirit of counsel will rest upon you. If you stand firm against vices, counting them as nothing even as you uproot them, you will have the spirit of fortitude. And if you are humble in heart and chaste in body, you will surely be able to be raised on high, strong enough to serve confidently in the spirit of knowledge. And if you add these virtues to your mind and body, without doubt there will rest on you the spirit of knowledge.

If you have fraternal compassion for your neighbors, if you offer hospitality, and if you are the steadfast helper of the poor and the afflicted, you will have the spirit of piety. And if your loyalty toward your father and your earthly lord leads you to respect and love them as well as the magnates and all your peers, old and young alike, and if you do not participate in insults to them or shameful contention against them, the spirit of the fear of God will certainly rest upon you.

You will find that Holy Spirit discussed in the book of Wisdom where it says, *The Spirit of the Lord hath filled the whole world.*[58] For, as the Highest sees fit, he surely *breatheth . . . where he will.*[59] The holy apostles were made drunk by the breath of this inspiration[60] when *they going forth preached everywhere,*[61] and they fulfilled their preaching by laying on their hands. By "hands" is meant the sacred gift left behind by the Holy Spirit. As the prophet writes, *the word of the Lord came by the hand of Aggeus the prophet,*[62] that is, the word of the Lord was in the hand of him who fulfilled it. About this word and its fulfillment, you may read in the Apocalypse. There it says, *Blessed is he who readeth* my words. It continues, *and keepeth those things which are written in it.*[63]

The gift of the Holy Spirit, as the blessed Apostle Paul says, renders great rewards to each one according to his merits. For he says, *To one indeed, by the Spirit, is given the word of wisdom: and to another, the word of knowledge,* and to another the insight of understanding *according to the same Spirit.*[64] *But all these things one and the same Spirit worketh, dividing to everyone according as he will,*[65] that is, the same one that is called God. For God is a spirit, as the Evangelist says, *God is a spirit, and they that adore him, must adore him in spirit and in truth.*[66]

So, my son, seek these virtues of the Lord in the Holy Spirit, and that great benefactor will grant them to you. For a certain great king and prophet said when he wished to be filled with the same spirit and prayed confidently for it, *Create a clean heart in me, O God: and renew a right spirit within my bowels.*[67] And again, *Take not thy holy spirit from me.*[68] In giving thanks for being filled with the Holy Spirit, he besought with deep feeling that it not be taken away, saying, *Strengthen me with a perfect spirit.*[69] If one as great as he, who lived so long before us, spoke so as he struggled on in the name of the Holy Spirit, what then should we say—we who can be compared on the ground of our merits but to a shadow of his example?

All the same I pray you, direct you, and ask of you that you too seek this in the Holy Spirit. If you consider well and *with all watchfulness keep thy heart*[70] pure, that right Spirit will be renewed in your bowels. If you speak well and keep your mouth free of evil *and thy lips from speaking guile,*[71] the Holy Spirit, the most worthy possession of him who receives it, will not fail you. And if you in turn carry out in worthy action that of which you have thought and spoken, you will surely be strengthened in this perfect spirit.

What further shall I say? I will close my homily appropriately briefly. If you live by thinking well and speaking well and acting well —*soberly, and justly,* chastely, and *godly in the world*[72]—and if you walk in the right Spirit and the Holy Spirit and the perfect Spirit,[73] in the holy and indivisible power of highest deity, so that you take your stand and reside there, you will be able to rest secure always and everywhere. In doing so, as the Spirit supports you with its gifts, you will be able to reach the heavenly kingdom.

5. *More on the same topic. Useful direction on various aspects of moral betterment.*

From our beginning, in turning the rashness of pride and the puffing-up of arrogance into their opposite, gentleness, we have followed a great plan. Now, with the help of the threefold grace of the Holy Spirit,[74] let us put up a strong seawall against what follows, waves beating all around us, by correcting our moral faults as if returning arrow for arrow.

It is written in a passage of a certain book: be strong in war and fight with the ancient serpent.[75] For the blessed Peter warns us about the struggle with this serpent, urging us to resist it manfully and saying: *Watch because your adversary the devil, as a roaring lion, goeth about seeking whom he may devour. Whom resist ye, strong in faith.*[76] You must keep watch, my son, and strive manfully in the accomplishment of good works, lest the true and holy redemption of the blood of God's son perish in you. Set virtues against vices, as I have said above, so that you may be found worthy to be protected *from the multitude of the workers of iniquity.*[77]

6. *On the same topic. Setting opposites against each other.*[78]

If, because of the persuasion of the devil, fornication or some other spur of the flesh should drive your heart to frenzy, set chastity against it, and remember the continence of the blessed patriarch Joseph, and of Daniel,[79] and of those others who faithfully maintained purity in spirit and body in respect to their lords and their neighbors. They were therefore found worthy to be saved and honored, gathered up by the Lord full of praise among the number of his saints. For as the Apostle says, *fornicators and adulterers God will judge.*[80] And the Psalmist says, for behold they who fornicate away from thee shall perish.[81] And the Apostle says likewise, *Every sin that man doth, is without the body; but he that committeth fornication, sinneth against his own body,*[82] and other comments of this sort.

Therefore, my son, flee fornication and keep your mind away from any prostitute. It is written, *Go not after thy lusts, but turn away from thy own will.*[83] Do not *give to thy soul* to fly away after her evil desires.[84] Surely, if you attend to one or another of these ills and if you consent to them, they will make you fall onto the sword and into the hands of your enemies. They will say with the Prophet, *Bow down, that we may go over you.*[85] May this not happen to you. But if those evils come and sting your mind through an angel of Satan sent against you,[86] fight them, pray, and say with the Psalmist, *Deliver not up to the beasts of the earth my soul, I beseech you, and forget not the soul of thy poor servant;*[87] *give me not the haughtiness of my eyes;*[88] *let not the lusts of the flesh take hold of me, and give me not over to a shameless and foolish mind.*[89]

The haughtiness of my eyes has, I think, not only an outer, corporeal sense but also an inner sense. For if it did not have inner meaning, this saying would be empty. *I have made a covenant with my eyes, that I would not so much as think upon a virgin,*[90] and many similar sayings in many places. You will find consolation in such great accounts so that you may, in petitioning God, escape the thrill of such embraces and the temptation of such turmoil. And although it is in the head that the eyes of the flesh are turned to desire, the struggle against such evils is fought within. For it is written of eyes turning in passionate desire that they perform their wrongful outrages carnally. *For death is come up through our windows,*[91] and again, *whosoever shall look on a woman to lust after her*[92] does so carnally.

As for those who adhere to continence and who crush beneath their heels the desire of the flesh, you find it written, *The light of the body is thy eye.* And *if thy eye be single, thy whole body shall be lightsome.*[93] He who said this, *Turn away my eyes that they may not behold vanity,*[94] and many things like it, wished that chastity be inviolable. For as learned men say, "chastity is the angelic life,"[95] and it makes whoever participates in it a citizen of heaven. "O," someone says, "how short, short indeed is that moment of fornication by which future life is lost! And how great is the strength and the enduring splendor of chastity, which makes a mortal man like a fellow citizen of the angels."[96]

For learned authors do not refuse sacred marriage to the union of the flesh,[97] but they try to root out from among us libidinous and wrongful fornication. For Enoch was chaste, and so were Noah, Abraham, Isaac, Jacob, Joseph, and Moses, and all the others who struggled to keep their hearts pure in Christ in the union of marriage.[98] And what more shall I say?

So my son, whether you keep your body in virginity, a resplendent gift, or in the chastity of the union of marriage, you will be free from the origin of this sin. Your mind will be *secure . . . like a continual feast*,[99] and will rest throughout all you do in all of the eight beatitudes. And there will be fulfilled in you in the company of other good men, as it is written, the worthy praise offered for many: take courage,[100] *blessed are the clean of heart, for they shall see God.*[101]

7. *That you be patient in mind and body.*

If, because of the plague of rancor, your heart seethes in wrath, control it as best you can. It is written, *anger resteth in the bosom of a fool.*[102] And so a certain author says in his poem:

The stupid man, he who lacks understanding, cannot speak,
Nor, breaking the tumble of words, can he ever
Keep silence; quick to anger,
Slow to make peace, he turns from bad to worse.[103]

May such never befall you, noble boy.

Anger is known to be harmful to the spirit in all good activity. Concerning this damaging wrath, the Psalmist says, as if of himself, *my eye is troubled with wrath.*[104] The Apostle says, *For the anger of man worketh not the justice of God.*[105] If such anger should come upon you, take charge of it lest it be victorious over you and tear your mind to pieces. Although it is only human to be angry, still—so that this evil not become an ingrained habit—trample it into the earth until it is totally destroyed. Lest anger afflict many souls, the Psalmist says warningly, *Be ye angry, and sin not.*[106] Such conquest over anger was the wish of him who spoke to those around him, beseeching them with his admonition to be gentle: *If it be possible, as much as is in you, have peace with all men.*[107] Concerning this peace, another says in his poem:

Peace holds back anger;
Quarreling fears peace.

> Secure peace
> Rests far and wide;
> Friendly concord
> Flies toward heaven.[108]

If anger climbs into the inner chamber of your spirit, my son, cast it away from you. *Give place to wrath, . . . be not overcome by evil, but overcome*[109] anger with peace. Recall the attitude of him who ruled almost six hundred thousand people and who we read was never disrupted by anger. It is written of him: he was a great man, *most faithful in all my house,*[110] and *a man exceeding meek above all men that dwelt upon earth.*[111] This means that he reached the height of goodness. If by himself he patiently sustained the ways of his own people, who were so many and who so greatly neglected their duty, what should it be for us and for those like us, among our lesser challenges, to act as he?

We find that the same man was so praised in holy Scriptures that he was found worthy to receive whatever he sought of the Lord. And because he performed his earthly struggle with consistent patience and gentleness of mind and body, because he always shone forth brightly in his generosity, mindful of the presence of the omnipotent, he spoke with God as a man with his friend.[112] Therefore he was found worthy to receive a great response from that great Lord. It is written of this man, *And the Lord was appeased from doing the evil which he had spoken against his people.*[113] The Lord said further to Moses, *I will do according to thy word.*[114]

What more shall I say of him? He was so calm in his mind that, clear-sighted, he never knew the darkness of confusion, and he kept all his teeth.[115] Undiminished in bodily strength and flourishing in charity up until the end of his life, passing his time without burden of grief, he controlled his anger. Always he sought after *the conditions of peace.*[116] Following the ways of truth day and night, he finished a life of great worth in peace. O how pleasant and wonderful are those courts where integrity of spirit rests peaceful through all things and leads the body unharmed to its heavenly goal!

I have presented this man as a model so that you may take pleasure in the thought of his gentleness as a sort of lesson for your own mind.

Many who restrain their own anger, and in their mildness bring about peace among others, are known to please God in their faith and purity of spirit. Great virtue is attributed to those who are patient. Such good effort concerned him who said, *The patient man is better than the valiant: and he that ruleth his spirit* with great patience in all things is better *than he that taketh cities.*[117]

8. *To overcome your faults with ease, read the eight beatitudes aloud, and keep them always in your heart.*

It is I, Dhuoda, who give you direction, my son William. I wish that, as you grow patiently in worthy virtues among those who fight alongside you, you may always be *slow to speak, and slow to anger.*[118] If you grow angry, do so without sin. May it never happen that our merciful God grows angry in turn with you or—and may this also never befall—that you stray in your anger from the true path.

Therefore I direct you that, with gentleness, justice, and holiness, you perform your worldly service to him who, admonishing his faithful ones to shine with patience, says, *In your patience you shall possess your souls.*[119] If you are patient, and if you restrain your thoughts and your tongue, you will be blessed. Your mind will be at peace, fearless everywhere, as if you were at a feast in the midst of many merrymaking companions. For it is written, *a secure mind is like a continual feast.*[120]

When you are well instructed by these and other examples, may you strive to act so peacefully that you may be found worthy to share the lot of blessedness with those of whom it is written, *Blessed are the peacemakers: for they shall be called the children of God.*[121] Surely a man should devote much effort to such a matter, so that—though he is the son of mortality—he may be found worthy to be called as well the son of the living God and to be established as the heir of that Lord's kingdom. If you are gentle and if you plow the furrow of good works, going forth always in honor, you will be found worthy to be joined with those of whom the Lord, granting a great inheritance for their praiseworthy manner, says, *Blessed are the meek: for they shall possess the land.*[122]

If you encounter a poor man, offer him as much help as you can, not only in words but also in deeds. I direct you likewise to offer generous hospitality to pilgrims, widows and orphans, children and indigents and to be quick to lift your hand to help those who you see are in need. As Scripture says, *we are sojourners, immigrants and strangers, as were all our fathers*[123] who passed upon the earth. Read Moses' admonition to the sons of Israel that they show brotherly compassion; he exhorted them strongly, saying: remember that *you also were strangers and pilgrims in the land of Egypt.*[124] Another man said of pilgrims and wayfarers, so that he might be their companion in his fraternal compassion and so that he might find others to be his successors in this great effort, *my door was open to the traveller.*[125] He said about orphans: I was the *father of orphans and the judge of widows.*[126] And again, *and the cause which I knew not, I searched out most diligently.*[127]

You must not fail to have pity for the poor, my son, for God often hears their voices, as the Psalmist says. He says, *The Lord hath heard the desire of the poor.*[128] And again, *This poor man cried, and the Lord heard him.*[129] For the poor man and the man in need cry out the Lord's name and praise him. We know that poverty and want are found not only among the least of men but also frequently, for many reasons, among the great. So it is that a rich man too may be in need. Why? Because his soul is wretchedly needy. And then there is the poor man who gathers riches with great ease. Or the rich man who envies the poor man, or the poor man who wishes to become rich, just as an unlettered man wishing to become learned may desire this completely but never accomplish it. Of such men a certain author says: "The rich and the poor man perish together, and are at once tortured by their need, the rich man because he does not give away what he has, and the poor man because he does not have it. When they sleep, they are oppressed by similar burdens: the former do not have the spirit of humility, nor do they find the blessed rest of the spirit of poverty."[130] They are restless and troubled for what is hateful to many. Someone says, *my soul hateth . . . a poor man that is proud: a rich man that is a liar.*[131]

Opinions vary about differences between the rich and other rich men, and between the poor and other poor men. It was a rich, distinguished man who said, *But I am a beggar and poor.*[132] And again, humbling himself the more, he said, *But I am a worm, and no man:*

the reproach . . . and the outcast of the people.[133] Then again, *woe is me, alas, my sojourning is prolonged*[134] too much. Setting aside his riches *with the consolation of the Holy Ghost,*[135] returning to himself, he said, *The Lord is my firmament, my refuge, and my deliverer,*[136] and he is always prompt in being *careful for me.*[137] Therefore I joyfully confess his praise in the words of this poem: *I will sing to the Lord, who giveth me good things.*[138] I will *sing to the name of the Lord the most high,*[139] that his law may be always fruitful in my mouth.[140]

If so great a man spoke of himself as least among the small, lowliest of all, what of us? He hoped in the Lord, and that bountiful liberator freed him from all dangers. Surely those who have come before us, our forefathers and predecessors who called out to the Lord on account of their many worthy merits and placing their hope in him, *were not confounded*[141] or led into disgrace but—as we believe—were filled with spiritual and material riches and in the end were saved. As the same author affirms, the houses of Abraham, Isaac, Israel, Moses, Aaron, and Levi, and others whose names *I am not worthy* to list or whose shoes to unfasten[142]—men who had hope in the Lord and called out to him with all their heart, whom he *brought . . . out of their distresses* and led safely *to the haven which they wished for*[143]—praised his greatness on earth and are blessed in the world to come. Confessing him, they say, *Praise ye the God of gods . . . the Lord of lords,*[144] praise him all *kings of the earth and all people,*[145] of all nations and languages,[146] for he is great and *good: for his mercy endureth* for time and eternity.[147] Since they and those who have come after them, believing as they did, confess and praise him, I urge you that you too love all the good things mentioned above and that, as an attentive reader and doer of good works, you strive to fulfill these last counsels, too, in the most worthy fashion.

Fear the Lord, and you will meet with such praise as the Psalmist offers. For he says, *Blessed is the man that feareth the Lord.*[148] As for whoever is found worthy to be filled with this fear, *His seed shall be mighty upon earth. . . . Glory and wealth shall be in his house* through all things, *and his justice* will gleam forth *for ever and ever.*[149] If I were able, I would will it that what was true for them be true for you as well. As it is, I wish and pray that it may come to pass for you, my boy.

Love purity, and you will be the companion of him who is bright and gleaming, more splendid than any other. A certain author says, "Love chastity, boy, and you will be pure of sin."[150] And another says: love chastity, young man: shining in it, you will give forth a rich fragrance. Pure of sin, you will cross the high clouds of heaven in your course.[151] Follow this path, and you will share with the pure of heart that blessedness of the spirit about which you may read above. In Sion you may see[152] him who said, *Blessed are the clean of heart, for they shall see God.*[153]

Love the poor, and gather them to you. Do your duty to them at all times in the spirit of mildness and gentleness, lest you forget fraternal compassion for those who are beneath you. Always let your nobility be clothed in a suppliant heart, in the poverty of the spirit. Then you will be able to listen untroubled and to share in the kingdom with those of whom it is written, *Blessed are the poor in spirit: for theirs is the kingdom of heaven.*[154]

Love justice, so that you may be recognized as just in legal matters. *For the Lord is just, and hath loved justice. He loves it always. His countenance* beholds *righteousness.*[155] Another man loved it greatly long ago, and he directed that it be loved when he said, *Love justice, you that are the judges of the earth.*[156] Yet another said, *if in very deed you speak justice, judge right things.*[157] It is written, *for with what judgment you judge, you shall be judged.*[158]

Therefore, my son William, avoid iniquity, love fairness, follow justice, and fear to hear the saying of the Psalmist: *he that loveth iniquity hateth his own soul.*[159] That Lord who is true and pure has given you a soul that is true, pure, and immortal, though in a fragile body. May it not befall you, then, to prepare evil snares for that soul, for the sake of desire for transient things, by doing or saying or consenting to acts of injustice or pitilessness. For many are tormented for the wrongdoings of others.

Be mindful, if you arrive at this point, of Elias and the rest. For a certain author says, "I sin with all sinners, if I do not correct them when I see them sinning."[160] And another says, *Lift not up the horn* to the sinner.[161] Whatever is passed over in lesser persons is demanded of those who are greater. Each iniquity or injustice returns to him who committed it. It is so among kings and dukes, and so also among bishops and other prelates who live badly or vainly and who not only perish for their own injustices but also cause others to fall headlong by allowing their wrongdoings. Such is described in these words: "In doing and consenting they accumulated equal punishment."[162] If persons who share the same faults do not correct each other, they are punished in the same fashion, tumbling to the depths.

A certain man used to pray, "Lord, do not let me, your servant, be separated from you, nor let me share in the sins of others."[163] Each man recognizes the magnitude of his own wrongdoing. As the blessed Apostle says, *See therefore, brethren, how you walk circumspectly.*[164] And again, *every one of you should know how to possess his vessel,*[165] that is his body. How, or in what way? He adds: in justice and in the sanctity of truth.[166]

My son, if you love justice and do not allow evil men to do evil deeds, you will be able to say confidently with the Psalmist, *I have hated the unjust, and have loved thy law.*[167] May you not share the fate of those about whom the Prophet spoke long ago, saying, *Woe to them that make wicked laws*[168] and who allow deceits and evil plots to be designed *to cast down the poor and needy, to kill the upright of heart.*[169] Such folk lust after wrongful things, and they are rightly punished. The Evangelist says of them, as they deserve, *And woe to them that are with child, and that give suck.*[170] The one who is pregnant is he who wrongly covets the things rightly belonging to another. He who gives suck, who does not rear his own, is he who possesses what he seized unjustly.

Such men have lived for only a short time and then are delivered up to the long death of hell. As the great prophet says: *They spend their days in wealth, and in a moment they go down to hell.*[171] How heavy and unbearable a transformation! Better for such a man not to have lived than to exist in such misery. What good is there in noble blood, my son, if one's body is corrupted by injustice, so that it grieves forever in its descent to putrefaction? It profits a man nothing, if he gains the world and loses himself,[172] for *the world passeth away, and the concupiscence thereof.*[173] Although a man may gleam with gold, gems, and purple, he goes to the darkness lowly and naked, taking nothing with him unless that he has lived well, piously, chastely, in a worthy fashion. But because we believe such to be true, I urge you that you always love justice and shun vice.

If you do so, you will be able to say with confidence to that good and true judge, *Thou art just, O Lord, and thy judgment is right.*[174] And again, *I know, O Lord, that thy judgments are equity,*[175] *all thy ways are truth,*[176] and therefore *I have done judgment and justice.*[177] In loving your law, I have always clung to hope.[178] As you thirst after justice with the blessed, your *soul shall be as a watered garden,* rich in *wine and oil.* In the enjoyment of beatitude, that soul will thirst no more.[179] Then you will easily find a place among them of whom it is said, *Blessed are they that hunger and thirst after justice: for they shall have their fill.*[180] These happy souls shall be satisfied, my son, with that food which does not perish but *which endureth unto everlasting* life.[181] They will eat that most worthy bread of which it is written, *Man ate the bread of angels;*[182] he who is ever filled *shall never thirst.*[183] Find pleasure in working for this bread, in investing yourself in good works.[184] As you eat it, you will be blessed in your activity and still more blessed in your rest. As you walk and as you stand still, all will be well with you; happiness will always remain in your house. Around your table, your sons will bless the Lord, praising him, like the offspring of a new plantation of olives.[185]

So be merciful. Reveal your mercy and your gentleness whenever you take part in the resolution of legal matters. For after judgment is given, that excellent mercy always finds its place.[186] The bountiful one who directs us says, *Be ye therefore merciful, as your Father also is merciful.*[187] For if you love mercy and make it the companion of your mind, you will be made blessed along with those of whom it is written, *Blessed are the merciful; for they shall obtain mercy.*[188] Show mercy as much as you are able even to the least of men, to those subject to you, and to those in need. Then you too may be found worthy to be treated mercifully by our good and merciful God. And be meek. In all your undertakings, hold yourself to the standard of meekness. As a certain poet says:

The meek man wears out his body;
His illustrious hand is the benefactor of souls,
And in his generosity he is beset by the sticky attentions of
    the court.[189]

60

Blessed are the meek.[190] Blessed are the gentle, for *they shall possess the land*[191]—not only on this earth, but also with a great future inheritance in God's temples.

As for all the wealth God grants you, use it to extend a generous hand. May no one attribute greed, *which is a serving of idols,*[192] to you. But if God grants something great or small to you, offer it to another who asks for it, according to his worth. Give so that you may receive. For it is written, *Blessed is he that understandeth concerning the needy,* and *blessed is he* who thinks of *the poor,*[193] for he finds praise in his lifetime and his works are thought great. As another author says, *he that giveth to the poor, shall not want.*[194] A just and generous man, although he passes from this world, will live afterward in endless glory and happiness.

Therefore, my son, *honor the Lord* before all else, as Solomon says, *with thy substance and . . . the first of all thy fruits,*[195] and give of your other wealth to the poor. Give so that, in the last judgment, you may be found worthy to ask with a calm, clear conscience: "Give, Lord, because I have given. Take pity, because I have taken pity." For the divine speech of the evangelist tells us, *Make unto you friends* of mammon, so that when you die *they may receive you into everlasting dwellings.*[196]

Hide your frequent acts of charity in the lap of the poor man, and he will pray for you to the Lord.[197] You have as your authority him who directs you and others, *Give, and it shall be given to you.*[198] Again, *give alms; and behold, all things are clean unto you.*[199] For as learned authors say, *alms deliver* the soul *from death, and will not suffer* it *to go into darkness.*[200] Why? Because, just as water puts out fire, so acts of charity extinguish sins.[201] And once they are extinguished, they are lost in darkness. Although the healing powers of charity are many, I wish you to make use of three among them frequently: first, to give to a needy man whatever you have or whatever he secretly asks of you; second, to forgive in Christ those who have done harm to you. For that good Lord and peacemaker said, *Forgive, and you shall be forgiven.*[202] And again: as you stand in prayer, be forgiving.[203] For he says too: If thou remember go to be reconciled.[204] Third, frequently correct those who err, with blows as well as words if need be.

It is written, *reprove, entreat, rebuke.*[205] This saying commands that you entreat the good and rebuke the evil. Its author says of the shameful: I shall *come to you with a rod.*[206] He says of the worthy: or I shall come to you in worthy fashion, as he says, *in the spirit of meekness.*[207] All along your path, when you catch sight of those who wander, lead them back to the way of truth as best you can. Then, broadly confident yourself, you will be able to practice the three species of almsgiving.

9. *That you help the poor as you are able.*

Pay heed even to the poor man who annoys you with his petition. It is written, *provoke not the poor man crying out.*[208] For he is troubled in his heart and cries out with his mouth; he wishes that what he utterly lacks be given to him. You must imagine, I urge you, that if you were yourself to have fallen into such profound need, you too would wish this to be given to you.

Just as appropriate response is required by evil deeds, so too in respect to honorable actions. For it is said of wrongs: do not to another what you do not wish done to you.[209] And it is written about response to worthy generosity, *All things therefore whatsoever you would that men should do to you, do you also to them.*[210] It is fitting that he who accepts at no cost another's goods should offer his own for free to the extent that he can. Therefore I direct you to minister with food and drink to the needy and with clothing to the naked. May each man give away with a smile what he knows is his. It is written, *Deal thy bread to the hungry, and bring the needy and the harbourless into thy house: when thou shalt see one naked, cover him, and despise not thy own flesh.*[211]

Here, the word "flesh" signifies the state of brotherhood in which all of us take our origin, as the first-made man himself said of her who was like him and joined to him, *This is now bone of my bones, flesh of my flesh.*[212] For "flesh," *caro,* takes its name from "to fall," *cadere,* in the sense and to the degree that the poor man as well as the rich may fall and rise again, but all are returned to dust in the end.[213] Hence it is just that those who acquire great things through their merits should offer material sustenance and aid to such lesser persons of whom they are aware. In fraternal compassion—for those who thirst, hunger, and are naked, to orphans and pilgrims, strangers and widows, and to little children and all the needy and oppressed—help them kindly, taking pity upon them whenever you see them. For if you do so, *then shall thy light break forth as the morning,*[214] and brightness shine upon your steps everywhere. Mercy and peace will never desert you, and everywhere, through all time, truth and justice shall go before thy face.[215]

Accompanied by these good works, you will then call upon the Lord, and he will hear you: *thou shalt cry, and he shall say, Here I am.*[216]

Book Five

1. *On being tested in various troubles.*

Troubles, sorrows, and difficult temptations follow close upon each other, in this life, in many ways. Such is the case for men of the spirit just as for men of the flesh. Men of the flesh feel sorrow about transitory things, and men of the spirit are troubled that they may lose heavenly things. *The sorrow of the world,* as the Apostle says, *worketh death,*[1] but spiritual sorrow leads toward eternal life and joy.

Some varieties of birds express their grief in song, with the pitch of their voices. What does this suggest, but that each of us mortals, following his respective path, should send forth a double lament from the heart? On the one hand each has failed in the good that he ought to do, and on the other hand he has acted perversely in loving that which he ought not. Human grief thus branches out in two directions,[2] unable to utter a clear song. Therefore we must battle against the sorrow that cripples us, and hold steadfastly to what benefits the soul. Spiritual sorrow is nobler than fleshly; it comes to the human heart for many reasons. Wise men say that thoughtful consideration of such spiritual grief is better than the attempt to forget its presence.

So, for instance, one such wise author says: as though we are *sorrowful, yet always rejoicing,* and again, as though we are needy, yet possessing all things.[3] When we say "as though," we mean not in reality; for what is real is not "as though." A man who has been dreaming says: It was as though I were riding a horse, as though I were running; as though at a banquet I held the drinking-vessels in my hands, along with the tableware and platters of fruit so delicious that they

65

tripled my appetite. Or it was as though I were riding horseback, jostling up and down. But when I was aroused from sleep there was nothing that I could see or hold; empty and weak, out of my mind and shaking, I remained entirely "as though." O, if it had been true, that which I met with my eyes, felt with my hand, stepped upon with my feet![4]

And O, our learned author says, if someone like me, now or in the future, should perceive this "as though" as true and be deluded by these images, he might run to the feast. But he would be dying as he ran. Such is the "as though" that is joy in the earthly things that the unwise and the neglectful must leave behind in this world. Nothing remains through their funeral chants but "as though."[5] Why? Because their goods pass away and only the damnation of their eternal death remains. For everything that pertains to those whose understanding is only of this world is understood by wise men, is it not, as "as though"? Pay attention to another author who says: I have seen everything under the sun and, lo, vanity, vanity of vanities, all is vanity.[6] There you see how "as though" is bound up with the sleep of vanity. Why? Because as the Psalmist says: *All the foolish of the heart were troubled. They . . . have all slumbered that mounted on horseback.*[7] When they have been awakened from sleep[8] they *have found nothing in their hands,*[9] and they have followed a path that they cannot retrace.

How heavy and unbroken a sleep will it be for those who have lived evilly and have tumbled toward the depths without benefit of repentance! What is there in them but "as though"? They have passed *as ships carrying fruits.*[10] They are like the straw that flowers in the morning and is burned at the dusk, already dry, hard and brittle. The Psalmist testifies this when he says, *all flesh is straw,* and its glory will seem like the flower of the field.[11] Although it seems to live long on this earth, it is as fragile as a web. It is short, and once it is cut it is destroyed forever. If this were not so, the blessed Job would not have said: *Man born of woman, living for a short time, is filled with many miseries. Who cometh forth like a flower, and is destroyed, and fleeth as a shadow, and never continueth in the same state.*[12] And lest man be unaware of the shortness of his duration, Job adds, *my skin is withered and drawn together,* and *my days have passed more swiftly than the web is cut by the weaver, and are consumed without any hope.*[13]

The happiness of the human condition is as fragile as this, and it is so short even for those who know it longest that—even if it extends a thousand years—its final day is still but a grain of sand. It is written: a thousand years in the sight of men, when they have perished, are *as yesterday, which is past.* For them their years are nothing in the flux of time, like a watch that passes vainly in the night.[14] As Scripture says: the life of man upon earth is but a trial.[15] Suddenly the "as though" is clear, and the truth is revealed to all. Then, lo, you have the "as though," and behold the truth. Why? Hear the Prophet, *My harp is turned to mourning, and my organ into the voice of those who weep.*[16] My singing, drowned in moaning, is only weeping. To him whose feet before were washed in butter, and for whom the rocks flowed with streams of oil,[17] whose many possessions grew and grew, and for whom thrones were set up in the marketplaces[18]—when all this was overturned—it was all different, taken away. He sat alone on the putrid dung-heap.[19] Worms, his only food, slithered about. What was clear to him as he lost his offspring, his children, but "as though"? What remained for him but pouring out with groans of grief that this was the truth? "As though" remained for him when all his grief was gone. The truth remained when, recovering what was his before, he faced the day happily, healthy and watchful, with the things that belonged to him.

For that is the truth, as we believe—that he ended his earthly time in peace, wholesome and pure, going happy and cleansed to his forefathers. He himself spoke of the negligent and the evildoers, recognizing the truth and the "as though" while he still lived in the secular world, saying of what befell such men: *They spend their days in wealth*: for there is the "as though." *In a moment they go down to hell*:[20] and there is the truth. There are more texts of this sort.

If the learned authors tell us that we must believe such things—and I urge you to do so—then there is no doubt that we must honor, fear, and above all love him *who taketh away the spirit of princes,*[21] so that each of them returns to the earth whence he came and then cannot even recognize his former place. The very earth, when it is returned to mud and dust, produces filthy worms. As this author says, *when a man shall die, he shall inherit serpents,*[22] and so forth.

Another writer says, *when a man sleeps in death and is stripped and consumed, I pray you where is he?*[23] Where? Without doubt, as learned authors say, he will be wherever he falls,[24] whether it be to the east, to the west, to the north, or to the south. Important meaning lies in these directions. What it is too long to explain through examples is easily expounded by those who are wise. For it is written: If a tree falls in one direction, *there shall it be*.[25] As anyone can understand, a tree is either good or bad and is known by the fruit it bears.[26] A beautiful, noble tree grows noble leaves and bears appropriate fruit. And so it is for a great man, great in faith. A learned man is found worthy to be filled with the Holy Spirit and to send forth leaves and fruit. He gives forth a sweet fragrance. His leaves are words, his fruit perception; or his leaves are understanding, his fruit action. The good tree puts forth good things, and the bad is handed over to the fire. It is written, *Every tree therefore that doth not yield good fruit, shall be cut down and cast into the fire.*[27]

For that true tree and that true, noble grapevine, our Lord Christ Jesus,[28] from whom the chosen trees rise up and send out their fronds, saw fit to choose such worthy branches as might bear beautiful fruit. He said, *I am the vine; you the branches.*[29] And again: I have chosen you from all the world, *that you should go, and should bring forth fruit; and your fruit should remain.*[30] *He that abideth in me, and I in him, the same beareth much fruit.*[31] I urge that you cling to that tree, my son, so that with the fruit of good works you can hold to him without fail and bear many fruits. Those who see these things and have firm faith in him are like a tree that is bountiful because it is planted near a stream of water.[32] Those who stretch their roots deep into the earth are not parched in the heat of summer.[33] Their leaves will always be green and fertile, and they will never fail to bear fruit. Why is this, my son? Because, as the Apostle says, *rooted and founded in charity*[34] by the welcoming grace of the Holy Spirit, they never fail to provide fruit for those around them.

So that you can know what sort of trees most frequently bear worthy fruit, hear again what the Apostle says: *the fruit of the Spirit is, charity, joy, peace, patience, benignity, goodness, longanimity. Mildness, faith, modesty, continency, chastity,*[35] sobriety, watchfulness, and shrewdness, and other like things. Since those who do these virtues' works are found worthy to enter the kingdom of God easily, plant their fruits in your mind and body, and bring them forth. Think upon them constantly, my son, so that, with the fruit and the perseverance of good works, you may be found worthy to be protected and comforted by the true tree.

2. On making amends, if you go astray.

If you should do something wrong, my son, or when you are sorrowful in spirit, hasten as best you can to improve your own self. Turn back to him who sees all things. Both in public and in your own mind, acknowledge yourself guilty and unworthy until you have made satisfaction. Say: "*The sins of my youth and my ignorances do not remember.*[36] I beg, Lord, that you *draw me not away* with my iniquities,[37] and do not in your anger perpetuate my evildoings even to the end. But come to my assistance with your accustomed forgiveness and generosity, because you are good."

Remember, my son, the words of the tax collector: "*O God, be merciful to me a sinner,*[38] for I am unhappy and unclean, unworthy to raise my wretched eyes to you, who are most pure. Why? Because the weight of my sins oppresses me, and I am not strong enough to raise my eyes, unless you, who alone are without sin, extend your hand to me and lift me up as I lie in the flood of danger. Raise me up, Lord, whom the lapse of sin has marred with stains; bring me light, blind as I am and covered by the shadows of darkness; release me, shackled by the chains of sin—you who have heard the thief's confession and have pardoned the deceits of the tax collector, who have assigned rewards to the just and have offered your pardon even to sinners, saying: *I desire not the death of the wicked, but that the wicked turn from his way, and live.*[39] Therefore I desire that I be converted to you, corrected of my faults, and that I adhere to your commandments, most just Father, with all my strength and all my effort."

If you try to set these and other good examples before your heart, sorrow—which is only "as though"—will pass away from you. Then truth[40]—that is, the joy that comes of the knowledge of future things —will take its place. Such a joy the *eye hath not seen, nor ear heard, neither hath it entered into the heart of man* ever! What great things— of what kind—*God hath prepared for them that love him*[41] with a whole heart! If you come to such joy, my son, no one will be able to separate you from it, and you will share with many others the possession of that great eternal blessedness of which is written, *your joy no man shall take from you.*[42] So that you may be found worthy to partake of such joy, I urge you constantly, my son, to keep yourself not only from sin of your own doing but also from the sins of others. Say with the Psalmist, *From my secret ones cleanse me, O Lord: and from those of others spare thy servant.*[43] What more shall I say?

3. *On various temptations, if they befall you.*

In difficulty, in persecution, in temptation, in hard and trying situations, in danger and in illness,[44] and in all the weakness by which the frail body is overwhelmed, show courage and wise preparedness. It is written, *With all watchfulness keep they heart.*[45] Strive with all your might that it remain guarded.

4. *If there is difficulty.*

If difficulty befalls you, my son, as I have said, bear up patiently. It is written, *tribulation worketh patience.*[46] For if you cry out in time of trouble with faith in God, he will hear you. Listen to the Prophet: *In my trouble I cried to the Lord.*[47] *Thou calledst upon me in affliction, and I delivered thee: I heard thee.*[48] *In an acceptable time . . . and in the day of salvation I have helped thee.*[49] Therefore, my son, when you come into difficulty, cry out and you will be found worthy to be heard. And when you have been heard you will be able to praise God confidently, saying, *In my trouble I called upon the Lord: and the Lord heard me, and enlarged me.*[50]

5. *On persecution.*

Have no anxiety about persecution, I beg you. It is written, *Blessed is the man that endureth temptation; for when he hath been proved, he shall receive the crown of life.*[51] And then, *Blessed are they that suffer persecution for justice's sake.* Again, *Blessed are ye when they shall revile you, and persecute you, and speak all that is evil against you, untruly, for my sake.*[52] If such befalls you for your sins, bear up patiently and suffer it in Christ.

6. *In hardship.*

If hardship comes to you, have faith and say, "God, *deliver me from my necessities.*"[53] You will one day be able to recover your prior rank, if the good Lord commands it. Remember Job and Tobias.

7. *In deprivation.*

Any deprivation is suffering. In such distress, in the suffering of deprivation, that man also struggled who said, *I am poor, and in labours from my youth: and being exalted have been humbled.*[54] Why? Because *thy terrors have troubled me.*[55] *Friend and neighbour thou hast put far from me, and my acquaintance.*[56] So that in the day of evils you may not be unmindful of good things,[57] I urge that you call out to the Lord your protector to help you in soul and body in such difficulties and trials as may befall you. Remember, my son, the troubles of Joseph, David, Daniel and Susannah, Shadrach, Meshach and Abednego, and those others who called out to the Lord in hardship. Not only were they heard, but they were restored to their prior rank with even higher favor.

8. *In illness.*

If illness should come to your body, neither yield to it nor allow it to make you sorrowful. The Lord's chastening brings comfort and health to the body and the soul. It is written, *My son, reject not the correction of the Lord: and do not faint when thou art chastised by him: for whom the Lord loveth, he chastiseth;*[58] *and he scourgeth every son whom he receiveth.*[59] The Lord stands as close to the one whom he chastises, in whom he is pleased, just as a father to his son. Many people, learned authors say, fall ill for their own good. Why? Because when they are healthy in body they never cease to think about plundering and luxury and other evildoings. So when God visits such men in his goodness, he takes pity on them.

There are some who grow sorrowful because of their great bodily health. That man struggled against such sadness who said: You have left me, God, you have left me, and you have not wished to come to me in this year.[60] And there are many others who rejoice in bodily illness. There was he, for instance, who understood illness as a benefit, saying: For when I am weak, then I am strong.[61] So that illness of this sort would not ever bring him sorrow, he said in adoration, with great feeling, *For I reckon that the sufferings of this time are not worthy to be compared with the glory to come, that shall be revealed in us.*[62] There are many, too, who have bodily health from God on account of their great merits. Think of the blessed Abraham, Moses, and so forth.

Health and illness have various effects in this world, as is often the case in human affairs. In some people either leads to glory, and in others to shame. Pilate and Herod were sickly,[63] and so were other agents of the devil,[64] but theirs were not simple illnesses. Rather they deserved not a simple punishment but double suffering, in body and in spirit. Of these and others like them the Prophet says: destroy them with double punishment,[65] Lord. On the other hand Lazarus, Peter's mother-in-law, and the servant of the centurion fell ill,[66] and so did others, but when they were sick it was not so that they might die but so that *the Son of God may be glorified*[67] among all who hear and believe. Of such individuals and others like them you find it written, "You have healed their illness, and their pains have gone away."[68] Why is this? Hear the Prophet, *Afflicted in a few things, in many they shall be well rewarded.*[69] And *all tears* shall be wiped away *from their eyes: and grief shall be no more, nor mourning . . . nor sorrow shall be any more, for the former things are passed away.*[70]

What we have said concerning the double meaning of difficulties, let us say also about the twofold meaning of earthly goods.[71] Someone says of the high rank of the saints, *The just shall shine, and shall run to and from like sparks among the reeds,*[72] and for all eternity they shall have two cloaks.[73] Why? Because the Lord has tested them and found them to be pure as silver and gold.[74] Therefore they will receive the kingdom of honor and the crown of distinction from the hand of God. Constantly I admonish you, my son, that you seek the glory of this dignity. If God should command that great health be given to you, I beg and urge that you use the health of the body as a foundation for the salvation of the soul. Read *Pastoral Care*[75] and you will understand.

9. *That you give glory to God in all circumstances.*

Whatever you receive that is worthy, useful, and appropriate for you, my son, attribute it to God, not to yourself as if you judged it to have happened on account of your own great merits. If you have some such benefit, give glory to God. It is written, *Not to us, O Lord, not to us; but to thy name give glory.*[76] For what does man have that he does not receive from outside himself? And if we receive such goods, why should we glory in them?[77] So I urge that you give highest praise, honor, and glory to him who is truly glorious. And if riches come to you, do not place your heart in them, for someday they pass away.

But if you wish to be truly rich, learn wisdom. Embrace it, resting in it always. It is written, *There is a treasure to be desired*[78] in the heart of the wise man. We must embrace that treasure and those riches. Robbers do not carry them away, and *thieves do not break through, nor steal.*[79] Whoever has spent earthly riches well can easily arrive at that true wealth of which I have written here. Abraham was rich, and so were his descendants Joseph, David, and Solomon, and he too who said, "You know, I have not eaten the bread of my desires."[80] Rich in years, these men flourished and grew strong far and wide in the poverty of the spirit, just as is written above, *Blessed are the poor in spirit.*[81] The end.

Book Six

1. *On the same topic, attaining the virtues brought to you by the seven gifts and the eight beatitudes.*

My intent here is to set forth and explain in turn those eight beatitudes linked, respectively, to the seven graces of the Holy Spirit,[1] which I have written about for you above. In doing so, I have seen fit to address myself to you, who are only a boy, in the childish terms appropriate to my own understanding. I have done so as if you were unable to eat solid food but could take in something only like milk.[2] Climbing little by little, as if on a stairway, you may then progress easily from lesser to greater things so that you can eat that heavenly food of which the Psalmist says, *O taste, and see that the Lord is sweet: blessed is the man that hopeth*[3] and trusteth in him, thinking of him always. Therefore I have not been so bold as to place these beatitudes in order according to the way that they appear in the gospel, my son. I am not capable of that, so I have presented them in a fashion suited to your few years, as I have said. I who am but as a child myself have given you milk rather than solid food,[4] for you are also a little one in Christ.

You must set forth, then, in the poverty of the spirit, so that you may arrive at him who is rich, from whom all just and holy riches come, without suffering and with a pure, clear conscience. In that way you may enter upon the fullness of the perfection of that man about whom the Prophet says, *Behold a man, the Orient is his name.*[5] That author says "the Orient" because he who is glorious in heaven has redeemed us with his precious blood, taking our poverty upon himself to enrich us with his own wealth.[6] That Lord commands that our name be written in heaven among his saints if we are found fitting and worthy. So the Lord says, *Be glad and rejoice, for your reward is very great before God,*[7] and again, *but rejoice in this, that your names are written in heaven.*[8]

2. *I direct you to be a perfect man.*

Blessed is that man who, on account of his worthy merits, wears down his feet in mud and dust as he walks upon the earth.[9] Already his name is enrolled in the heavenly kingdom.

If you wish to know what sort of a man that may be, my son, or what sort of virtues he had that he should be so enriched with many earthly honors and the possession and enjoyment of God's kingdom and tabernacle, hear the Prophet asking: "*Lord, who shall dwell in thy tabernacle? or who shall rest in thy holy hill?*[10] I wish that you might show me." We have heard this as a question, but we should know and understand fully what the Lord's answer was.

3. *I show you how you can be, with God's help.*

The Lord says: first, *he that walketh without blemish*; second, *he that worketh justice*; third, *he that speaketh truth*; fourth, *he who hath not used deceit in his tongue*; fifth, he who hath not *done evil to his neighbor*; sixth, *he that sweareth to his neighbour and deceiveth not*; seventh, *he that hath not put out his money to usury*; eighth, he who hath not *taken up a reproach against his neighbors*; ninth, he who hath not *taken bribes against the innocent*;[11] tenth, he who has borne injuries patiently; eleventh, he who is *innocent in hands*; twelfth, he who is *clean of heart*[12] and chaste in body; thirteenth, he *that could have transgressed, and hath not transgressed*; fourteenth, he that *could do evil things, and hath not done them*;[13] fifteenth, he who stretched out his hand to whatever poor man he could.[14]

Such a man can dwell secure in the lofty tabernacles of God,[15] and for that reason *are his goods established in the Lord*;[16] in his sight *the malignant is brought to nothing.* Persevering in worthy works, he always *glorifieth them that fear the Lord.*[17]

4. *On the ways of calculating the number seven.*

For the seven gifts of the Holy Spirit and the eight beatitudes of the

Gospels add up to thrice five. The computist says:[18] seven once is seven, seven twice fourteen. And again: four once is four, four twice is eight. To these add seven, and they come to fifteen. A certain wise man says about these sums, *Give a portion to seven and also to eight*.[19]

Again: seven twice is fourteen. Add one, and that makes fifteen. And then you say: seven sevens are forty-nine. Add one, and you get fifty. When you continually add one to a multiple you quickly arrive at a round number. Again you say: seven elevens are seventy-seven, and seven seventies are four hundred ninety. Again you say: three threes are nine. Add one and that makes ten, and in the same way you can reach ten thousand.

What the differences are among these various calculations, my son, is too long to explain step by step, but I will set it forth for you briefly so that you are at least familiar with this sort of reasoning. The number that is called seven sevens invites each one of us to fuller satisfaction. Add one and the sum represents the grace of the Holy Spirit correcting us toward the remission of our sins and changing us through our amends. This number confirms the high rejoicing of the fiftieth psalm and of the jubilee year, since the word "jubilee" means remission and absolution. You sing about such rejoicing, I believe, the many times you offer this psalm: *Restore unto me the joy of thy salvation, and strengthen me with a perfect spirit*.[20]

Likewise, you should understand seven elevens as the correction of the body joined to the satisfaction of the mind. Again, know always that seven times seventy means to set aside the injury that you feel that others have done you. For this is what the highest prince of the apostles said: *Lord, how often shall my brother offend against me, and I forgive him? till seven times?*[21] And the Lord said to him, *I say not to thee, till seven times; but till seventy times seven times*.[22] He who can calculate these things says that seven times seventy amounts to four hundred ninety. It is as if the Lord said: that man is more than someone close to you, or more than just anyone; he is your brother. He may sin against you not only in deeds, but also in words. Still, if it is possible, forgive him for them and for still more. The good Lord says: *For if you will forgive men their offenses, your heavenly Father will forgive you also your offenses*.[23]

In these seven gifts of the creator[24] and eight beatitudes, which together form fifteen steps, I urge you, my son, to climb thoughtfully, little by little. Then at the number one hundred, as you go from left to right, you may easily reach the summit of perfection without having come to harm. For people who are learned in calculation count to ninety-nine on the joints of their left hands, but when one arrives at one hundred, the left hand fails the task. One may happily reach one hundred on the right.[25] It is written about counting on both hands, *His left hand under my head, and his right hand shall embrace me.*[26] What is meant by the left hand, my son, but the present life in which we all toil? And what by the right hand but that holy, worthy, heavenly fatherland? May Christ, who thunders from the highest heaven, see fit to extend your sweet life a long time, so that in the number of your good years you reach the ninety-nine of those who can calculate. May he who gave Ezechias fifteen more years[27] see fit to extend your lifetime, and after many years pass, may you reach that happy one hundred. *As it shall be the will of God in heaven so be it done.*[28] Amen.

By the sustaining grace of Holy Trinity, which endures through time without end, amen. These beatitudes come to a close through the saving grace of the Holy Spirit, concluding thus, *rejoice in this, that your names are written in heaven.*[29] May the good Lord, glorious king and magnificent conqueror of this world, bring you in gladness, my son, to this joy and this kingdom. Amen.

Book Seven

1. *On the same topic. Special direction of great usefulness.*

I have helped you here as much as I have been able to set in order your earthly experience, so that you may act calmly and confidently, without dishonor, while you serve as a warrior or embrace the contemplative life.[1] Now, from this point on, I will act as your mother in spirit as well as in body, continually instructing you how to direct your soul's service to perfection with God's help, so that every day you may be reborn in Christ.

Learned authors tell us that each man has two births, one the birth of the flesh, the other of the spirit—but the spiritual is nobler than the fleshly. Among the human race one cannot exist without the other, and since the two belong together, the Apostle says, "With them we live, and without them we cannot live."[2] Although the sense of this passage does not exactly fit my meaning, I wish you to understand it according to my context here.

2. *I wish that you be strong in your first birth.*

As for the first birth, there is no one who does not know that each one of us is born with sin.

You will find something of an explanation below of how this is shown in the calculations of the Greeks. I urge you to learn it, for such knowledge is worthy of the wisest men and enlightens us greatly in all matters.

3. *I direct you to be steadfast in your second birth.*

Concerning the second birth, that is, the spiritual, the gospel says, *unless a man be born again.*[3] It says of the first birth, *That which is born of the flesh, is flesh.*[4] And it adds about the second birth, *And that which is born of the spirit, is spirit.*[5] Concerning the way in which one man may be the father of many others in this second birth, hear the Apostle, *My little children, of whom I am in labor again, until Christ be formed in you* the more securely.[6] And again, *by the gospel,* I say, *I have begotten you.*[7] In terms of this second birth many men have many, many offspring. Or read about that blessed lady who was the mother of the young Celsus,[8] and blessed Augusta who was the mother of Saint Symphorian, citizen of Autun,[9] how they were mothers to their children in both the first birth and the second birth in Christ.[10] Many men as well—in those times, now, and always—have begotten their sons again and again "by the Gospel" in the holy church, in their teaching of its holy doctrines and the example of their conversion to good works.

4. *On the first and second deaths.*[11]

The first death is the crossing-over of the body either to the good or—may this never happen—in the other direction. The second death is the death of the soul. Although death befalls man in many ways, it always retains these aspects.

5. *I call you to consider the first death.*

No man can escape the first, as the Psalmist says, *Who is the man that shall live, and not see death?*[12] This means no man. A certain father said when his son had passed away from the earth, his eyes closed: "This is the way of all flesh. I will follow him, and when I have gone I will not return."[13] Another spoke thus to his subjects when he was on the brink of death: *"Behold this day I am going the way of all the earth.* Listen to what I say, and to the words of my mouth, because I call upon the name of the Lord."[14]

6. *Struggle to escape the second death.*

But a man can escape the second death, if he wishes and if he has struggled worthily. For someone says: *He that shall overcome, shall not be harmed by the second death*,[15] but *I will make him a pillar in my temple . . . and I will write upon him* my name and *the name of the city of . . . the new Jerusalem*,[16] *and will make thee as a signet*[17] in my sight. Then *I will give to eat of the tree of life, which is in the paradise of my God.*[18] Blessed is he who so struggles among the disruptions of this world that he is found worthy to be heaped with such honor. Unmindful of death, he will find eternal life with the saints. So that you may enter that company, I enjoin for you, my son, and so that your will may grow in Christ, read and pray often.[19]

Book Eight

1. *I direct you to grow strong through reading and prayer.*
   In holy reading you will learn how you must pray and what you should avoid, be wary of, or seek out—what you should do in all matters. Everything will be clear to you there. The Apostle directs us regarding how often we pray: *Pray without ceasing.*[1] Another author says: let not the pupil of thy eye keep silent.[2] Must we pray constantly, and must our eyes always cry out? No, this is what that passage means: whatever good you do in this world will be a constant prayer to the Lord on your behalf. If you pour out tears to the Lord for your wrongdoings and for those of others, your eyes will surely call out and pray to the Lord. In this regard I urge you that, when you read and pray in a most worthy fashion, you always keep your mind watchful and alert, pure and clean. Read and pray so that he who hears all[3] may see fit to listen to you as well.

2. *On the past, the present, and the future.*[4]
   Pray for the past, the present, and the future. Pray for the past, if you have been neglectful, that you may finally forget this; for present evils, that you may always escape them; for the future, that you may beware those evils and that they not continue to pursue you there.

3. *I suggest how you may pray for all the ranks of the clergy.*
   Pray as best you can for all the ranks of the clergy.

4. *For bishops and priests.*

Pray first for the bishops and all the priests, that they may pour forth to God pure and worthy prayers for you and for all the people.

5. *For kings and others of the highest rank.*

Pray for kings and all those of the highest ranks, that they may uphold the universal church's firm belief in Christ and that they may maintain the earthly realm in such peace that they eventually reach the heavenly kingdom.

6. *For your own lord.*

And pray for your own lord,[5] that God may strengthen him in body and in soul so that he accounts his troubles as nothing. May he always be illustrious—prosperous and prudent, watchful and eminent, happy in every endeavor. And may he see fit to direct the vigor of your youth with respect and fear, with prudence and love, to the highest rank.

7. *I direct you to pray constantly for your father.*

As for your father, I urge that you pray for him frequently, constantly, and that you ask the various ranks of the clergy to pray for him, so that God may grant him peace and harmony with all men—if that can be[6]—as long as he lives. Pray too that the Lord cause his strong mind, joined as it is with his great patience, to prevail everywhere, and pray that God bring him after the end of this present life to the heavenly kingdom through the fruit of his penitence and the richness of his charity. Amen.

8. *On the same topic, for all the following.*

You must pray too for those who oppose you and make difficulty for you and insult you, so that *the peace of God, which surpasseth all understanding, keep your hearts and minds*[7] and make them peaceful in word and deed. Then finally they may all, with one mind and one voice, glorify that God who reigns in heaven. Amen.

Pray for travelers, that God may show them the best route;[8] for those who sail, that they may happily disembark at a safe port; for the sick, that God may give them the salvation of the soul and the healing of the body and so that, rising up from the bed of their sickness, they may praise and bless the Lord in churches; for those who are afflicted, for those in difficulty, for the needy, and for those suffering trials, and for all sorts of others whom I have omitted here. Read the prayers for Holy Friday, the day of our Lord's passion, and there you will find how you must pray for all the people.[9]

9. *End with the words, "and for all the holy people of God."*
It says in one of these prayers, after many other things, "and for all the holy people of God."

10. *That you pray for all the faithful who have died.*
Pray too for all the faithful who have died, that the good Christ may come to their aid, deigning to gather their souls to the bosom of Abraham, so that they may receive rest and refreshment in the future with the saints. As learned authors say,[10] we offer alms to the dead in three ways when we make these offerings.

11. *For those who were truly good.*
For those who were truly good, we offer thanks.

12. *For those who were not truly good.*[11]
For those who were not truly good, propitiation.

13. *Here you will find something appropriate to offer for those who were unworthy.*
And still we must pray for those who were truly evil and unworthy. Why? Because even if it is not to their own souls' advantage, still they receive some comfort from the merits of others,[12] that is, of the poor. And nevertheless, although it is uncertain on whose behalf God accepts any gift of prayer, we must offer it for all, and it must be welcomed by the faithful ministers of the church of God, except perhaps when it is offered for those—may this not happen—who stray from the faith of Holy Trinity[13] or who, in desperation, end their days evilly. For God knows the hearts of all and the end of all his creatures.[14]

We must not despair of anyone, but implore God faithfully for all. Perhaps the good Lord may take pity on his creature at the time of his judgment, for the Apostle offered his most worthy compassion not only for the souls of the faithful but also for those who were not truly faithful. He lamented again and again, groaning for them, *I mourn* that much more for those who *sinned before, and have not done penance*.[15] For I think that he offered lament for those who sinned before the flood and perished in the rising of the waters, or surely for those who sinned under the law and met bitter death before doing penance. The Apostle says too, *whosoever have sinned in the law, shall be judged by the law*.[16]

We must pray for everyone, especially for those who have received the grace of baptism, even if they have failed in some way and have not done penance before the time of their death. What should we offer for them but double lamentation and frequent prayer? A certain spirit answered the query of an old man: "For those of us who have not known the law, nor ever received the grace of baptism, our punishment will be a bit more bearable, as if he said: *No man hath hired us*.[17] But those who, knowing God's power and the faith of Holy Trinity, have received the grace of baptism and after this acknowledgment have finished their days without doing penance, they will feel harsher torments." Then the old man said, "And what is your punishment?" The voice replied: "As far as heaven is from earth, so far is there fire over my head and under my feet. I and others like me stand in the midst. But those others whom I mention are underneath my feet in the depths of hell. They feel the most profound torments." Then the old man began to lament with groaning, saying, "Woe the day in which man transgressed the commandment of God," and then he went away.[18]

What more shall I say, my son? We must tremble before this statement. For I think that the blessed David saw himself as liberated in his spirit from this abyss when he said, *thou hast delivered my soul out of the lower hell*.[19] The rich man too, when he was first in torment, offered these few words, *for I have five brethren*.[20] And everyone knows what answer he received. If someone has sinned and has not corrected himself, what will become of him? Hear the Evangelist, *Bind him hands and feet, and cast him into the exterior darkness*.[21] I pray that you never hear such a sentence—but you must always correct yourself lest it befall.

We must pray for those who stumble and fall, that they rise back up, and for those who are standing, that they not stumble. Of those who are standing the Apostle says, *he that thinketh himself to stand, let him take heed lest he fall.*[22] What do I say about the others? I wish that you consider this for your own sake, and if—may it not happen— you fall after stumbling in some matter, do not despair, but correct yourself and place your trust in him of whom the Apostle says, *Rise thou that sleepest, and arise from the dead: and Christ shall enlighten thee.*[23] If you do awaken with the help of the Highest, do not cease to direct others that they too be roused. We must pray for the living and even more for the dead, that they may rise up in Christ. We must maintain this attitude toward the living so that they remember that they are about to die and that they must pray for themselves as if they were to live again. For if the Apostle grieved for those he did not know, as he said, what ought we to do for those immediately around us?

We must pray for everyone, especially for those who have received Christ's faith. And we must pray especially frequently not only for strangers but also for members of our own families, that is, for those nearest us and for those less closely related.[24] I say this so that I may achieve my own desire. Myself about to die, I direct you to pray for all the dead, especially those from whom you draw your earthly origin.

14. *Pray for the dead relations of your father.*

Pray for your father's relations, who handed down their goods to him in legitimate inheritance. You will find written down at the end of the chapters of this book who they were and what their names were.[25] Although Scripture says one man will rejoice in the goods of another,[26] their legacy has not gone to others, as I said before, but your lord and father, Bernard, has charge of it.

Pray for those who possessed this legacy to the extent that they have left it behind; and pray that you who are living may enjoy it long and happily. For I believe that if you struggle on behalf of the good Lord humbly, as is worthy, he will enrich you too with the transient honors of this inheritance. And if—should almighty God grant it in his mercy—your father should command that you be enriched by that patrimony,[27] then pray the more, as best you can, that heavenly reward come to the souls of those who possessed all these earthly goods. Because of his many pressing obligations, your father does not do so now himself. You must then pray constantly for their souls while you have the ability and the opportunity.

15. *For the late lord Theoderic.*

You must not forget your obligation, my son, to him who adopted you as his son in Christ at the font of rebirth, taking you from my arms. His name, while he lived, was the lord Theoderic—but now he is dead. He would have been your foster-father and your loving supporter in all things, if it had been permitted to him. But the bosom of Abraham received him, as we believe. Leaving you behind in this world as if you were his own firstborn child, he committed all his goods to his master and our lord,[28] so that they might be able to profit you in all things. Therefore pray often for him, as much as you can, whenever you have the chance—and especially when you are with other good men. Do so at the night office and at matins and at vespers and at the other canonical hours, and indeed at all times and all places, for the sake of his sins in case he acted in any way unjustly and has not repented for eternity. Command that sacrifice be made to the Lord on his behalf, through the prayers of holy priests and the distribution of alms to the poor.

When you pour out your prayers to God for him, begin by saying the following verses: "eternal rest"; "may his soul rest in good things"; "he will be just in eternal memory"; or whatever prayer you know better. When you have completed this, say the prayer: "Lord, may you see fit to place the body and the soul of thy servant Theoderic in the bosom of Abraham, Isaac, and Jacob, so that when the day you are revealed arrives, you may command him to be brought back to life among the saints and your chosen ones, through our Lord."[29]

16. *And again, pray for all the dead, that they rest in peace.*

See to it that the ceremonies of masses and sacrifices be offered on a regular basis not only for him but also for all the faithful who have died. No prayer is better for this purpose than the offering of sacrifice. For we read about the strong man Judas: *It is therefore a holy and wholesome thought to pray for the dead, that they may be loosed from sins.*[30] May they rest in peace. Amen.

88

17. *On the same topic, especially for you.*

And so, my son, I urge and direct you here, especially regarding that soul of holy memory whom I have just mentioned. As for the rest, be comforted in the Lord and in his great power. In your life in this world *bless God at all times: and desire of him to direct thy ways, and that all of thy counsels may abide in him* always.[31] May he who blessed the house of Abraham, Isaac, and Jacob, Moses and Levi, see fit to exercise his power over you for your salvation, so that you may be found worthy to have a place, with those whom I have mentioned, in his kingdom without end. Amen.

Book Nine

1. *On counting.*

The knowledge in this little book is partly derived from several other books, but my loving intent here has been to refashion their content in a manner appropriate to your age.[1] You may thus be led up to the height of perfection in fifteen steps.[2] I wish that, as your earthly time increases with God's help, so too the number of these steps may grow as you ponder them in your understanding.

2. *About the letters* ADAM *and their meanings.*[3]

Just as five times three make fifteen, so fifteen times three make forty-five. Add one, and that makes forty-six. It is this total that, expressed in Greek numerals, makes up the letters of the word *Adam*. For *A*, alpha, which is the east, is one; *D*, delta, which is the west, is four; and again *A*, alpha, which is the north as well, is one; *M*, moida, is the south, for forty.[4]

Adam reached out through his sons in all four of the world's directions. For one and four and one and twice four fives make forty-six. These numbers add up to the same number of days as the number of years in which the house of the Lord was restored in Jerusalem, that is, forty and six. For the Lord, wishing that it be completed in this very number of days, said to the Jews, *Destroy this temple, and in three days I will raise it up.*[5] And they replied, *Six and forty years was this temple in building; and wilt thou raise it up in three days?*[6] But he spoke of the temple of his body,[7] as if he said, "Destroy through my passion what I have taken on from your own origin, so that you may

91

hear: *Behold the Man,*[8] and I will raise it up in three days through the power of my divinity." The Prophet had spoken of these three days long before, saying, *He will revive us after two days: on the third day he will raise us up.*[9]

3. *About the thrice-five blessings that are yours always.*

Just as one and two and three and four make ten, so ten and twenty and thirty and forty make one hundred. And one hundred and two hundred and three hundred and four hundred add up to the number one thousand. One thousand and two thousand and three thousand and four thousand are ten thousand. You can, if you wish, go still higher: a hundred thousand and two hundred thousand and three hundred thousand and four hundred thousand amount to a million.

In each of these elements of calculation is contained a great and perfect number. For in one is represented he who is called God, since, as the Prophet says, *thou alone art the most high over all the earth.*[10] In two are the two testaments or the two commandments, that is, love of God and love of neighbor. In three another perfect, threefold number is signified, for he who firmly believes in it will be saved. In four are contained the four directions of the world, or the four columns [11] according to which the universal gospel is preached throughout the earth. In five are understood the five wise women, who arrived with the five senses of their bodies at a doubly bright perfection, in the whiteness of their virginity and of their chastity.[12]

In six, understand the six urns that empty through the six ages of time.[13] In these good men and bad are mixed together. Read and find out, and steep yourself to your profit in the good wine of Falernum.[14] In seven, as it says above, are the seven candelabra or lamps lighting the house of the Lord.[15] In eight, recognize the eight souls who were saved in the flooding of the waters—or those in the ark, that is, the church, who are renewed through the waters of baptism and found worthy to receive the eighth degree of beatitude as their victor's palm.[16] Nine represents the nine enduring orders.[17] In ten is meant the tenth order, which we confess and believe will be restored according to the sayings of the holy Fathers.[18] And there are still more interpretations of these numbers.

4. *On the same topic.*

We believe that, from the first-made man to the last who is to be saved at the end of the earth, all of them must be gathered up so that, as I have said above, the order of the angels may be replenished according to God's law.[19] In this restoration not only the Gentiles but also the generations of the Israelites must be saved, as Scripture says: *when the fullness of the Gentiles should come in. And so all Israel should be saved.*[20] May this salvation come to you in future time. Amen.

What further should I say to you on the subject of numerical calculation, my son William? All the numbers to ten add up, revealing good things, on only three fingers; and one can count up to one hundred and one thousand with all the joints and parts of the fingers of learned men; and up to a million is expressed through a variety of gestures for the salvation of all human beings, for a thousand thousands is the most perfect number of all.[21] If this were not the case, certain brothers would not have raised their voices to their sister, directing her with urgency, *Thou art our sister, mayest thou increase to thousands of thousands.*[22] If it is so among the weaker sex, what about the male?

May the omnipotent Father, in whom all the calculations mentioned above are worthily fulfilled, give you his blessing † according to the direction of the holy Fathers to their children, and according to the prayer of Isaac and Rebecca for Jacob. *May he cause you to increase and multiply in virtue.*[23] Amen.

5. *May he give you abundance from the dew of the heaven and the fatness of the earth.*[24] Amen. May grain and wine and oil and everything else pour forth richly for you. May the Lord be your helper and your strong defender against all enemies. Just as in the prayer of that man who offered it for those beneath him,[25] I am beside you in all things, my noble boy.

6. *Blessed shalt thou be in the city, and blessed in the field.*[26] Be blessed in the court, blessed with your father and blessed with your brother, blessed with great men and blessed with the small, blessed with lords and blessed with those who are younger than you, blessed with the chaste and blessed with the continent. May you be blessed with those

who are serious and those who stay watchful as they ought. And may the fruits of your lands be blessed. Blessed be your youth, your *coming in and going out.*[27] When you arrive at *old age and grey hairs,*[28] may you happily arrive from the struggle for salvation at the gate of souls with that thousand thousand. Amen.

Book Ten

1. *On the age you have attained.*

1) You have now reached four times four years.
If my second son too were of this age,
I would have another copy of this little book made for him.

2) And if in twice as many years and half again
I were to see your image,
I would write to you of more difficult things, and in more words.

3) But because the time of my parting hastens,
And the suffering of pains everywhere wears my body down,
I have in haste gathered this book for your benefit and your brother's.

4) Knowing that I cannot reach that time I have mentioned,
I urge you to taste this as if it were the food of your mouth,
Like a sweetened drink mixed with grain.

5) For the time at which I came to your father,
Or when you were born of us into this earthly world—
All this is known to us according to the dates of the months.

6) From the first line of this little book
To its last syllable, know that
All this is written for your salvation.

7) To find what is included here,
Read the chapter headings
So that you may easily take up what follows.

8) All the verses here—above and below, with all the rest—
I have dictated for the good of your spirit and your body.
I never cease directing you to read them aloud and keep them in your
heart.

2. On the verses I have begun with the letters of your name.[1]

1) So that you may flourish and be strong, best of children,
Do not hesitate to read the things I have spoken,
Written down, and addressed to you.[2]
There you will easily find what is pleasing for you.

2) God's word is living.[3] Seek it out.
Diligently study its sacred learning.
For your mind will be filled with great joy
Throughout all time.

3) May that great and strong king, the good, bright Lord,
Deign to nurture your mind through all that befalls you,
My young son. May he protect you and defend you
In every hour.

4) May you be humble of mind and chaste
Of body, ready to do good service,
So that you can readily accommodate yourself to all,
Both great and small.

5) Foremost, fear and love the Lord God
With all your mind and heart, and all your strength,
And then honor your father
In every way.[4]

6) As for that bountiful descendant of a line,
Scion of his race and lineage,
Him who shines in his great deeds—
Never hesitate to serve him constantly.[5]

7) Love the great magnates; esteem
Those who are first in the court, and act as the equal of those of low
degree.

Join yourself to those of good will, and take care
   Not to yield to the proud and the evil.

8) Always hold in honor the rightly constituted ministers of the divine rites,
Those who are worthy of the prelate's status.
With simple sincerity, commend yourself always with outstretched hands
   To those who keep the altars.

9) Help widows and orphans often,
And be generous to pilgrims with food and drink,
Prepare lodgings for them, and extend your hand with
   Clothing for the naked.

10) Be a strong and fair judge in legal matters,
Never take a bribe from anyone,
Nor oppress anyone. For he who has been your benefactor
   Will repay you.

11) Generous in gift giving, always watchful and prudent,
Agreeable to all, with a winning manner,
Profoundly joyful—such a countenance
   Will always be yours.

12) There is one who weighs out, who gives out in one direction or another.
He returns for the merits of all what their deeds deserve,
Granting the greatest reward, the stars of heaven,[6]
   For words and works.

13) And so, my noble son, seek diligently.
Take care to hasten to receive
Such great rewards, and turn away your eyes
   From the fires of blackened wood.

14) Although you count to your flourishing youth
Only four times four years' growth,[7]
Your tender limbs grow older
   As you travel your course.

15) It seems very far from me,
Wishing as I do to see the shape of your face—

If strength were given me, still my merits
Are not enough to win it.

16) May you live for him who made you
With a clear mind, and join the worthy company of his servants,
So that you may rise again in joy
After your course is ended.

17) Although my mind is wrapped in shadows,
Nevertheless I urge this, that you constantly read
The pages of this little book written out above,
And that you fix them in your mind.

18) With God's help these verses end,
Now that eight years have twice gone by,
At the beginning of December, feast of St. Andrew,
The season of the coming of the Word.

The verses end.

3. *A postscript on public life.*

Here the words of this little book conclude.[8] I have dictated them with an eager mind and have had them copied down for your benefit, as a model for you.

For I wish and urge that, when with God's help you have grown to manhood, you may arrange your household well, in appropriate order. As is written of another man who lived in this fashion, a man *like the most tender little worm of the wood,*[9] perform all the duties of your public life with loyalty, in a well-ordered fashion.

As for whether I survive to that time when I may see this with my own eyes, I am uncertain—uncertain in my own merits, uncertain in my strength, battered as I am among the waves in my frail toil. Although such is what I am, all things are possible for the Almighty. It is not in man's power to do his own will, rather whatever men accomplish is according to God's will. In the words of Scripture, *it is not of him that willeth, nor of him that runneth, but of God that showeth mercy.*[10] Now, trusting in him, I say nothing else but *as it shall be the will of God in heaven so it be done.*[11] Amen.

98

4. *Returning to myself, I grieve.*

The sweetness of my great love for you and my desire for your beauty have made me all but forget my own situation. I wish now, *the doors being shut,*[12] to return to my own self. But because I am not worthy to be numbered among those who are mentioned above,[13] I still ask that you—among the innumerable people who may do so—pray without ceasing for the remedy of my soul on account of your special feeling for me, which can be measured.

You know how much, because of my continual illnesses and other circumstances, I have suffered all these things and others like them in my fragile body—according to the saying of a certain man, *in perils from my own nation, in perils from the Gentiles*[14]—because of my pitiful merits. With God's help and because of your father, Bernard, I have at last confidently escaped these dangers, but my mind still turns back to that rescue. In the past I have often been lax in the praise of God, and instead of doing what I should in the seven hours of the divine office, I have been slothful seven times seven ways.[15] That is why, with a humble heart and with all my strength, I pray that I may take my pleasure in continually beseeching God for my sins and my transgressions. May he deign to raise even me into heaven, shattered and heavy though I am.

And since you see me as I live in the world, strive with watchful heart—not only in vigils and prayer but also in alms to the poor—that I may be found worthy, once I am liberated from the flesh and from the bonds of my sins, to be freely received by the good Lord who judges us.

Your frequent prayer and that of others is necessary to me now. It will be more and more so in time to come if, as I believe, my moment is upon me. In my great fear and grief about what the future may bring me, my mind casts about in every direction. And I am unsure how, on the basis of my merits, I may be able to be set free in the end. Why? Because I have sinned in thought and in speech. Ill words themselves lead to evil deeds. Nevertheless I will not despair of the mercy of God. I do not despair now and I will never despair. I leave no other such as you to survive me, noble boy, to struggle on my behalf as you do and as many may do for me because of you, so that I may finally come to salvation.

99

I acknowledge that, to defend the interests of my lord and master Bernard, and so that my service to him might not weaken in the March and elsewhere[16]—so that he not abandon you and me, as some men do—I know that I have gone greatly into debt. To respond to great necessities, I have frequently borrowed great sums, not only from Christians but also from Jews.[17] To the extent that I have been able, I have repaid them. To the extent that I can in the future, I will always do so. But if there is still something to pay after I die, I ask and I beg you to take care in seeking out my creditors. When you find them, make sure that everything is paid off either from my own resources, if any remain, or from your assets—what you have now or what you eventually acquire through just means, with God's help.

What more shall I say? As for your little brother, I have above directed you time and again concerning what you should do for him. What I ask now is that he too, if he reaches the age of manhood, deign to pray for me. I direct both of you, as if you were together here before me, to have the offering of the sacrifice and the presentation of the host made often on my behalf.

Then, when my redeemer commands that I depart this world, he will see fit to prepare refreshment for me. And if this transpires through your prayers and the worthy prayers of others, he who is called God will bring me into heaven in the company of his saints.

This handbook ends here. Amen. Thanks be to God.

5. *Names of the dead.*

Here, briefly, are the names of those persons whom I failed to mention above. They are William, Cunigund, Gerberge, Witburgis, Theoderic, Gotzhelm, Guarnarius, Rothlindis.[18]

Other members of your lineage still flourish in this world with God's help. It is entirely at the will of him who made them to summon them too. Son, what should you do in regard to them but say with the Psalmist, *we that live bless the Lord: from this time now and for ever?*[19]

When a member of your family passes on, this does not befall except through God's power. When the Lord so commands, as in the case of your uncle the lord Aribert, you who survive must effect that his name be written down among the others, and you must pray for him.

6. I ask that you write this epitaph on my grave.[20]

When I too have reached the end of my days, see to it that my name as well be written down among the names of those dead persons. What I wish and what I yearn for with all my might, as though it were happening now, is that you order the following verses to be cut in the stone of the place where I am buried, on the slab that hides my body. Then those who see this epitaph on my burial place may pour out worthy prayers to God for my unworthy self.

And as for any other who may someday read the handbook you now peruse, may he too ponder the words that follow here so that he may commend me to God's salvation as if I were buried beneath these words.

Find here, reader, the verses of my epitaph:[21]

† D † M †[22]

Formed of earth, in this tomb
Lies the earthly body of Dhuoda.
  Great king, receive her.

The surrounding earth has received in its depths
The flimsy filth of which she was made.
  Kind king, grant her favor.

The darkness of the tomb, bathed with her sorrow,
Is all that remains to her.
  You, king, absolve her failings.

You, man or woman, old or young, who walk back and forth
In this place, I ask you, say this:
  Holy one, great one, release her chains.

Bound in the dark tomb by bitter death,
Closed in, she has finished life in earth's filth.
  You, king, spare her sins.

So that the dark serpent
Not carry away her soul, say in prayer:
  Merciful God, come to her aid.

Let no one walk away without reading this.

101

I beseech all that they pray, saying:
   Give her peace, gentle father,

And, merciful one, command that she at least be enriched
With your saints by your perpetual light.
Let her receive your amen after her death.

   α † ω^{23}

Book Eleven[1]

1. *How to choose from among the Psalms.*

I have directed you above to observe the seven hours of the divine office. Now, with the Lord's help, I stand beside you as your instructor in which Psalms you should appropriately recite on various occasions.

The singing of Psalms, when it is done with the heart's concentration, prepares for our omnipotent God a way to enter in, infusing those who intently meditate with the mystery of prophecy or the grace of compunction. Whence it is written, *The sacrifice of praise shall glorify me.*[2] Thus the path to Jesus is shown in the sacrifice of divine praise, for when we pour forth compunction in the singing of Psalms we prepare in our hearts the road by which we come to Jesus. Indeed it is a worthy thing for the mind to wash itself clean of all the things of the present as much as possible and to fasten upon divine, heavenly, spiritual things so that those heavenly things may be revealed to it. There is nothing in this mortal life by which we can fasten ourselves to God more closely than by the divine praise of Psalm singing. For no mortal man can explain the power of the Psalms either in words or in his own mind.

If you concentrate intently upon the Psalms and arrive at a spiritual understanding of them, you will find the incarnation of the Lord's Word, as well as his passion, resurrection, and ascension.

If you concentrate upon them intently, you will find in the Psalms a prayer so intimate that you could never imagine it on your own.

You will find in the Psalms an intimate confession of your sins and full petition for the Lord's divine mercy.

You will find too in the Psalms the intimate thank-offering for all things that come to you.

And in the Psalms you will confess your weakness and wretchedness and call God's mercy upon you. For you will find all the virtues in the Psalms if God finds you worthy to reveal to you their secrets.

If you wish to do penance and make confession for your sins, and to ask forgiveness for your faults, concentrate as best you can not on saying the words quickly but on considering and pondering them. Recite the seven Psalms of David that begin, two of them, *O Lord, in thy indignation*, and two more, *Lord, hear my voice, Blessed are they*, and then *Have mercy upon me, O God*, and *Out of the depths*;[3] and you will swiftly come to God's forgiveness.

If you wish to brighten your mind with spiritual joy and gladness, recite with an eager spirit the Psalms that begin *Hear, O Lord, my justice, To thee, Lord, have I lifted up, O God, by thy name, May God have mercy on us, O God, come to my assistance, In thee, Lord, have I hoped*, and also *Incline . . . O Lord*;[4] then you will be able swiftly and confidently to achieve God's mercy.

If you wish to praise the omnipotent God, and to know even a little bit about him who has deigned to grant the majesty of all his gifts to the human race from the beginning of the world, then recite those Psalms whose title is "Alleluia" and that begin *I have cried to [the] Lord, Praise ye the Lord, Praise ye the Lord*, and *Bless the Lord, O my soul*.[5] You will offer almighty God a sweet gift of grain and honey if you continually praise and magnify him with these Psalms.

If you are afflicted by various trials and constrained on all sides by human or spiritual temptations, if you feel abandoned by God— who in this way abandons many of his saints in order to test them— and if in this trouble you seem to face a temptation greater than you can bear, recite within your own spirit those Psalms that begin *God, my God, look upon me, Hear, O God, my suppliction, Hear, O God, my prayer when I make supplication to thee*, and *Save me, O Lord*;[6] and he will come to your aid immediately, so that you can endure the temptation that you suffer.

If your earthly life weighs upon you, if your spirit finds delight in contemplating your heavenly fatherland and looking upon the omnipotent God with burning desire, recite these Psalms with an attentive spirit: *As the hart, How lovely . . . Lord, My God to thee at break of day*;[7] and the merciful God will swiftly console your mind.

If you feel that you have been abandoned by God in your trials, recite these psalms with a contrite heart: *How long, O Lord, O God, with our ears, Have mercy on me, O God, Hear, O God, my prayer and despise not, In you, O Lord, have I hoped*;[8] and God at once will make you happy in all your hardships.

After you have found rest, in time of prosperity, recite these Psalms in God's praise: *I will bless the Lord, Bless the Lord, O my soul, and let all, I will extol thee, O God my king.*[9] And in any time, either of prosperity or adversity, always sing the hymn of the three boys.[10] No mortal man can explain the power of this hymn, in which every creature is invited to praise the creator.

If you wish to occupy yourself within your own spirit in divine praise and in heavenly precepts and commands, recite this Psalm: *Blessed are the undefiled in the way.*[11] Even if you are still contemplating and studying the power of this Psalm at the end of your life, you will never—I think—be able to understand it perfectly. There is no verse in it in which the way of the Lord, his law, his mandates or teaching, his words, his sentences or judgments, or his sayings are not mentioned. And therefore you need not waste your effort on other books.

In the psalter alone you have the material for reading, studying, and learning up until the end of your life. In it the prophets, the gospels, and all the books of the apostles and other holy men are set forth and written down so that we may understand them in a spiritual sense. There you will find the prophecies of the Lord's first and second coming. You will find the incarnation and the passion, the resurrection and the Lord's ascension, and all the virtue of the divine sayings. If you study it within your own spirit, you will arrive at the marrow of inner understanding through the grace of God.[12]

Do not think of omitting, when you have completed the seven daily hours, the hymn "We praise you, Lord," or the creed that is written: "Whoever wishes."[13]

Because the recitation of the Psalms has such and so many powers, my son William, I urge and direct that you recite them constantly, for yourself, for your father, for all the living, for those persons who have stood lovingly by you, for all the faithful who are dead, and for those whose commemoration is written down here or who you command be added. And do not hesitate to recite the Psalms that you choose for the remedy of my soul, so that when my last day and the end of my life come for me, I may be found worthy to be raised up to heaven on the right with those good folk whose actions have been worthy, not on the left with the impious.

2.

Return frequently to this little book. Farewell, noble boy, and always be strong in Christ. † This little book was begun in the second year after the death of Louis, the late emperor, two days before the Kalends of December, on the feast of St. Andrew,[14] at the beginning of the holy season of the Lord's Advent. With God's help it was finished four days before the Nones of February, the feast of the Purification of the holy and glorious Mary,[15] always virgin, under the favorable reign of Christ and in the hope for a God-given king.[16]

Reader, if you are found worthy to see Christ in eternal happiness, pray for that Dhuoda who is mentioned above.

Thanks be to God, the handbook for William ends here in the word of the gospel: *It is consummated.*[17]

NOTES AND BIBLIOGRAPHY

ABBREVIATIONS

AASS   Acta sanctorum. Ed. Jean Bolland et al.
Paris, 1863–.

CC   Corpus christianorum, series latina.
Turnholt: Brepols, 1953–.

CSEL   Corpus scriptorum ecclesiasticorum
latinorum. Vienna, 1866–.

MGH   Monumenta germaniae historica.
Hanover, 1823–.
PAC:Poetae latini aevi carolini.
SS:Scriptores.
SSRM:Scriptores rerum merovingicarum.
SSRG:Scriptores rerum germanicarum
in usum scholarum.

PL   Patrologia cursus completus, series
latina. Ed. J.-P. Migne. Paris, 1844–64.

Notes

ACKNOWLEDGMENTS

1   A new corrected and modified edition of *Manuel pour mon fils* is being prepared.

INTRODUCTION

1   This and subsequent parenthetical references give the book and chapter titles or numbers used in the *Handbook for William* translation below and in the definitive edition: Dhuoda, *Manuel pour mon fils*, ed. Pierre Riché, trans. Bernard de Vrégille and Claude Mondésert, Sources chrétiennes 225 (Paris: Editions du Cerf, 1975), hereafter cited as Riché, Dhuoda.

2   For a compelling survey of Dhuoda's times and a rich bibliography on the aftermath of Louis the Pious's reign, see Rosamond McKitterick, *The Frankish Kingdoms under the Carolingians, 751–987* (London: Longman, 1983), esp. 106–99.

3   Bernard was accused, in contemporary chronicles, both of conspiracy and of adultery with Louis's second wife, Judith. Riché disbelieves these rumors (intro. to Dhuoda, 18).

4   Dhuoda recounts to her son the circumstances of her marriage in her prologue ("Preface"). Riché suggests that both she and Bernard may have been collateral relations of the Carolingians, as were many of the retainers of ninth-century kings (intro. to Dhuoda, 17–24).

5   See Peter Dronke's vivid reconstruction of Dhuoda's experience: *Women Writers of the Middle Ages: A Critical Study of Texts from Perpetua (†203) to Marguerite Porete (†1310)* (Cambridge: Cambridge University Press, 1984), 37–38.

109

6   Suzanne Fonay Wemple notes that Dhuoda's authority in Bernard's territo-
     ries was unexceptional as a woman's role among great Carolingian families:
     Women in Frankish Society: Marriage and the Cloister, 500–900 (Philadel-
     phia: University of Pennsylvania Press, 1985), 98–99.

7   Riché, intro. to Dhuoda, 17–21. For a lively, if old-fashioned, account of Ber-
     nard's troubles and exploits, see Eleanor Shipley Duckett, *Carolingian Por-
     traits: A Study in the Ninth Century* (Ann Arbor: University of Michigan
     Press, 1962), 37–41. Among Dhuoda's contemporaries, Nithard gives the best-
     detailed version of Bernard's ascendancy and subsequent difficulties, includ-
     ing his sister Gerberga's drowning as a witch: *Histories*, in Bernhard Walter
     Scholz, trans., *Carolingian Chronicles: Royal Frankish Annals and Nithard's
     Histories* (Ann Arbor: University of Michigan Press, 1970), 121, 131–35, 145–
     46, 156. Joachim Wollasch's study of Bernard's lineage as typical of Carolin-
     gian family structures and self-awareness offers a balanced overview of the
     activities of Dhuoda's husband: "Eine adlige Familie des frühen Mittelalters:
     Ihr Selbstverständnis und ihre Wirklichkeit," *Archiv für Kirchengeschichte* 39
     (1957): 163–67.

8   Riché, intro. to Dhuoda, 18–19.

9   See also Scholz, 156.

10   Riché reviews Bernard's family history and summarizes relevant bibliogra-
     phy (intro. to Dhuoda, 17–21). See also Constance B. Bouchard's detailed dis-
     cussion of the lineage of the dukes of Septimania and Aquitaine: "Family
     Structure and Family Consciousness among the Aristocracy in the Ninth to
     Eleventh Centuries," *Francia* 16 (1986): 641–44, 653–58.

11   Riché, intro. to Dhuoda, 21–24.

12   The ninth-century record of William of Gellone's life is an important source
     for the religious life of ninth-century nobles: *Vita de sancto Willelmo duce
     postea monacho Gellonensi in Gallia*, AASS, May 6, 809–22.

13   J. M. Wallace-Hadrill, *The Barbarian West, 400–1000* (London: Hutchinson's
     University Press, 1952), 125.

14   Riché stresses the uniqueness of Dhuoda's work (intro. to Dhuoda, 14).

15   Dhuoda, *L'éducation carolingienne: Le Manuel de Dhuoda (843)*, ed. Edouard
     Bondurand (Paris, 1887).

16   André Vernet, "Un nouveau manuscrit du 'Manuel' de Dhuoda (Barcelone,
     Biblioteca Central 569)," *Bibliothèque de l'école des chartes* 114 (1956): 20–
     44.

17   Riché, preface to Dhuoda.

18   For a recent assessment of Dhuoda's work and its authenticity, see Y. Bess-
      mertny, "Le monde vu par une femme noble au IXe siècle: Le perception du
      monde dans l'aristocratie carolingienne," *Moyen Age* 93 (1987): 162–84. This
      article, translated by M. Van Hemelrijck, had appeared in Russian in 1982. See
      also Dronke, 36.

19   Pierre Riché, "Les bibliothèques de trois aristocrates laics carolingiens,"
      Moyen Age 69 (1963): 87–104.

20   Riché, intro. to Dhuoda, 17–24; Bouchard, "Family Structure," 651–58.

21   Dronke, 40–41, 49–54.

22   Bouchard, "Family Structure," 642.

23   Rosamond McKitterick, *The Carolingians and the Written Word* (Cambridge:
      Cambridge University Press, 1989), 223–25.

24   Riché explains his division of the text into chapters and books, the latter his
      own notion rather than the manuscripts' evidence (intro. to Dhuoda, 53).

25   Dhuoda stresses that her work is as suitable for a young reader as milk is for
      a child (6.1). Her closing poem states that she would have written a different
      book for an older son (10.1).

26   See Riché's table of Dhuoda's textual citations and allusions (Dhuoda, 375–85).
      See also Myra Ellen Bowers's introductory remarks on Dhuoda's sources: in
      Dhuoda, "The *Liber Manualis* of Dhuoda: Advice of a Ninth-Century Mother
      for Her Sons," ed. and trans. Myra Ellen Bowers (Ph.D. diss., Catholic Univer-
      sity, 1977), xxx–xxxviii.

27   Riché, intro. to Dhuoda, 32; idem, "Les bibliothèques," 103–4; idem, *Les
      écoles et l'enseignement dans l'occident chrétien de la fin du Ve siècle au
      milieu du XIe siècle* (Paris: Aubier Montaigne, 1979), 286–305. M.L.W. Laist-
      ner's work remains the standard English survey of Carolingian education, up-
      dated rather than superseded by Riché's work: *Thought and Letters in Western
      Europe: A.D. 500 to 900* (Ithaca, N.Y.: Cornell University Press, 1957), 197–
      224.

28   Riché, intro. to Dhuoda, 35. For the centrality of the Bible to Carolingian learn-
      ing, see also Beryl Smalley, *The Study of the Bible in the Middle Ages* (Notre
      Dame, Ind.: University of Notre Dame Press, 1964), 37.

29   Riché, Dhuoda, 376–78. The author shared this attribution of the book of
      Psalms with medievals generally.

30   Bessmertny, 163, assembles bibliography for, then effectively counters, the
      argument that Dhuoda commissioned rather than composed the handbook.

31   Riché, intro. to Dhuoda, 11–15. See also Laistner, 252–57; Ritamary Bradley,

"Backgrounds of the Title *Speculum* in Medieval Literature," *Speculum* 29 (1954): 100–103, 108; Bessmertny, 165–66.

32 Riché, intro. to Dhuoda, 13–15. See also Bessmertny, 173, 179.

33 Dhuoda sets forth a program for William's prayer in Book 8 and borrows much from Alcuin's guide to the Psalms in Book 11 (see notes below). Bowers, xxxiv–xxxviii, notes Dhuoda's close awareness of the text of Benedict's Rule, as well as of contemporary Benedictine practice.

34 Compare Exod. 20:10.

35 Dhuoda explicitly states that royal authority is widely understood as the highest on earth, and she opposes this interpretation (3.2).

36 JoAnn McNamara and Suzanne F. Wemple, "Sanctity and Power: The Dual Pursuit of Medieval Women," in *Becoming Visible: Women in European History*, ed. Renate Bridenthal and Claudia Koonz (Boston: Houghton Mifflin, 1977), 101.

37 See McKitterick, *Frankish Kingdoms*, 71–72, 124.

38 See, for instance, Dronke, 40–41.

39 Riché, intro. to Dhuoda, 12.

40 Bowers, v–vi; Dronke, 40–41; Riché, intro. to Dhuoda, 14; Wemple, 98–99.

41 Helmut Beumann, "Topos und Gedankengefüge bei Einhard," *Archiv für Kulturgeschichte* 33 (1951): 340–45.

42 See Bowers, xxxiv–xxxviii.

43 Compare 2 Kings 1:25–27.

44 See, again, Bouchard's description of family structures and inheritance patterns as male-dominated ("Family Structure," 643).

45 Riché, intro. to Dhuoda, 21. See also Wollasch, 165–67.

46 Wollasch, 156–57.

47 Nelson, "Les femmes," 475.

48 See Bouchard, "Family Structure," 656.

49 Wemple, 194–95.

50 Scholz, 174.

51 Bowers, xxix–xxxi.

52 A lively discussion of these editions' relative merits has followed their appearance and has produced further suggestions for emendation and interpretation of the text. Compare Heinz Antony, "Korruptel oder Lemma? Die Problemmatik der Lexicographie auf dem Hintergrund der Editionen," *Mittellateinisches Jahrbuch* 16 (1981): 289–90, 332–33; idem, "Edition und Lexicographie: Zur Zuverlässigkeit kritischer Apparate," *Deutsches Archiv für Erforschung des*

Mittelalters 37 (1981): 774–75. See also Bengt Löfstedt, "Zu Dhuodas Liber Manualis," *Arctos* 15 (1981): 67–83; Lieven Van Acker, "Quelques suggestions à propos du texte du *Liber manualis* de Dhuoda," in *Hommages à Jozef Vermans*, ed. Freddy Decreus and Carl Deroux, Collection Latomus 193 (Brussels: Latomus, 1986), 319–27.

53 Compare Bowers, xxx.

54 Bowers, xxxiv–xxxviii.

55 Riché, intro. to Dhuoda, 41–45; idem, *Les écoles*, 299–300. Compare Dronke, 36–37.

56 For a recent discussion, see Peter Godman, ed., *Poetry of the Carolingian Renaissance* (Norman: University of Oklahoma Press, 1985), 51–53.

57 Riché, intro. to Dhuoda, 38, 41–45. For a survey of the linguistic context of Dhuoda's work, see Christine Mohrmann, *Latin vulgaire, latin des chrétiens, latin médiéval* (Paris: C. Klincksieck, 1955), esp. 46–50. Compare Roger Wright, *Late Latin and Early Romance in Spain and Carolingian France*, ARCA Classical and Medieval Texts, Papers and Monographs 8 (Liverpool: F. Cairns, 1982), 104–44.

58 Riché, intro. to Dhuoda, 53.

59 See esp. Van Acker, 319–20.

60 Riché, intro. to Dhuoda, 45–50.

PROLOGUE

1 Dhuoda begins by describing her own work as threefold, reflecting the trinity of the one Christian God—Father, Son, and Holy Spirit. In doing so, she affirms her adherence to this central element in Catholic doctrine.

All of the terms Dhuoda uses to describe her work identify it as part of the long tradition, extending from Augustine in the fourth century through Erasmus in the sixteenth, of the moral handbook—*enchiridion* or *speculum* ("mirror")—for lay Christians.

As Riché's comment on this passage points out (Dhuoda, 66 n. 1), Dhuoda's work follows less neat a plan than she outlines here. If her first two books amount to a "rule" for comportment before God, the third to a "model" for behavior among men, and the fourth to a "handbook" for William's inner life, such organization is extremely loose. The metaphor of "branching" is in any case one Dhuoda likes, for she returns to it to describe the patterns of human sorrow in Book 5.1.

2 Dhuoda means Paul, whose epistolary remains marked him, for medieval

113

Christians, as the most important of the apostles of Jesus.

3   1 Pet. 5:6.

4   Dan. 7:14.

5   Dhuoda's belief that all the Psalms were written by David, the shepherd boy who became the king of Israel, is an important aspect of her interpretation of their texts as well as of the nature of worldly power.

6   Ps. 143:7.

7   Ezek. 3:22.

8   Compare Ezek. 3:14.

9   Luke 1:66.

10 When Dhuoda refers to the "Fathers," she often means specifically the Fathers of the Latin church, most importantly Ambrose, Jerome, Augustine, and Gregory the Great. Sometimes she means more generally scriptural figures or famous personalities in the history of the church. Compare Riché's note on this usage (Dhuoda, 68 n. 4).

11 Dhuoda here exhibits a bit of Greek window dressing, using *scopon* for "destination"; she will, as Riché notes (Dhuoda, 69 nn. 5–6), return to this theme in Book 3.11. The synonym Dhuoda offers for "end," *senito*, must be garbled in its manuscript transmission or must have been garbled in her source. This passage is evidence of Dhuoda's great desire to demonstrate more learning than she could effectively command.

12 Rom. 13:12.

13 Compare John 8:12, 9:4–5, 11:9.

14 1 Cor. 3:6.

15 2 Tim. 4:7.

16 John 19:30.

17 As Riché notes (Dhuoda, 71 n. 4), Dhuoda may here refer to the trilingual inscription traditionally attributed to the cross: compare John 19:20. Although she attempts some Greek, she certainly knows no Hebrew.

18 Dhuoda begins her work again and again, as if shyly.

19 As Riché notes (Dhuoda, 72 n.1), Dhuoda's usage for writing here denotes scribal rather than authorial activity. She does not mean to say that the present work is not her own. Here again, at the same time, she recalls the image of a mirror, which she used in opening her prologue.

20 In Book 10.4 Dhuoda will enjoin William especially strongly to pray for her soul.

21 The following verses form an acrostic, a fashionable form among Carolingian

poets. The first letters of each Latin couplet spell DHUODA DILECTO FILIO VVILHELMO SALUTEM LEGE, or "Dhuoda sends greeting to her beloved son William. Read on."

The author's verses are rhythmic rather than quantitative, as was classical poetry. The meter of the verses is intended to reflect the dignity of their subject. For a translation of this acrostic poem, see Godman, *Poetry of the Carolingian Renaissance*, 275–77. For a discussion of Dhuoda's verse, see Godman's introduction, 51–52.

22 References to appropriate deserts were frequent in Christian funerary inscriptions, as Riché remarks (Dhuoda, 75 n. 1).

23 Dhuoda perhaps means the Virgin Mary, as Riché suggests (Dhuoda, 75 n. 2). Although the Virgin was revered as early as the ninth century as a sympathetic helper of human beings, she was not preeminent in this role until the twelfth century. It is therefore interesting that Dhuoda seems here to call on the mother of Christ. Her reference may be evidence that the Virgin was more important in women's than in men's piety in the Carolingian period.

24 Compare Isa. 40:12.

25 Dhuoda quotes material from the lives of Christian saints only infrequently. Here she means to refer, as well, to Old and New Testament figures.

26 In her fourth book, Dhuoda will describe the opposition of virtues and vices. As Riché notes (Dhuoda, 76 n. 1), the four virtues to which Dhuoda here refers are justice, courage, prudence, and temperance.

27 Dhuoda repeatedly mentions the uniqueness of her devotion to William, as Riché notes (Dhuoda, 77 n. 2); see Books 1.7, 10.4.

28 Compare Dan. 3:100.

29 Compare Ps. 23:1.

30 Dhuoda here mentions the Greek equivalent of the Latin *M*, the initial letter of her last verse. Again, her knowledge of Greek is purely superficial. See Riché (Dhuoda, 79 n. 2).

31 Compare 2 Cor. 11:23.

32 Wisd. 10:21.

33 Dhuoda here plays in a distinctly feminine fashion on the image of the mirror, *speculum*, also a literary genre embracing works such as her own handbook on moral education. Characteristically, she uses an ostensibly humble—even comical—illustration, but she does so in a fashion that affirms the significance of a woman's point of view in this important genre.

34 Compare Gen. 1:7.

35   Dhuoda here first advances a theme she will expound throughout her work—that William must demonstrate virtue both on earth and toward God. Soul and body, heaven and earth: the dialectical experience of a human being living in time and bound for eternity is an essential tension in her work, as in all Christian texts.

36   The marriage of Bernard and Dhuoda at the Carolingian capital, Aachen, suggests that they were children of families of great importance.

37   The year was 826.

38   Dhuoda here refers directly to the civil wars among Louis the Pious's sons, wars in which her husband was an important player and that were responsible for the sad disruption of her family at the time she wrote the present text.

39   Louis the Pious died in 840, late in his sixties, so Dhuoda's comment is merely a polite commonplace. As Riché notes (Dhuoda, 85 n. 5), Louis in fact reigned slightly less than twenty-eight years.

40   The year was 841. It is possible, given the long period between the births of Dhuoda's two sons, that she saw little of her husband in the interim. Bernard was heavily involved in politics and warfare across Frankish dominions throughout their marriage.

41   As Riché notes (Dhuoda, 85 n. 7), nothing else is known of this Elefantus—nor does Dhuoda reveal any further knowledge of the fate of her younger son. The matter-of-factness with which she describes this separation is belied by her following paragraph, in which she describes the length of the separation and her grief over it.

42   Dhuoda's dismay over her husband's actions toward her and her children adds ambivalence and irony to her arguments for the patriarchal ordering of family and society.

43   Compare Ps. 118:155.

44   Compare Job 30:16.

45   William had been entrusted to the emperor Louis the Pious's youngest son, Charles (later known as "the Bald"), both for William's own advancement and for Bernard's security, after the battle of Fontenoy in 841.

46   Matt. 6:33.

BOOK I

1   Dhuoda's language here echoes the verse section of her prologue, as Riché notes (Dhuoda, 97 n. 1).

2   Dhuoda here clearly states that she hopes for more than a family audience for

her work. This assertion has been generally ignored in the widely accepted characterization of her little book as intensely personal.

3   Dhuoda's self-depreciation here, as Riché points out (Dhuoda, 97 n. 4), takes the form of a Carolingian commonplace.

4   Gen. 18:27.

5   The author here reflects the notion, common to antiquity and the Middle Ages, of decline from an earlier—in this case biblical and apostolic—time.

6   3 Kings 8:27.

7   Exod. 33:13.

8   Exod. 33:20.

9   Acts 17:28.

10   Compare Mark 7:28, Matt. 15:27. Here Dhuoda adds an image for herself as *catula*, "female puppy," among the male puppies, *catuli* or *catelli*, of the New Testament. Characteristically, she at once affirms and depreciates the level of her own insight into spiritual matters.

11   Compare Luke 24:45.

12   Compare Ps. 118:125.

13   Ps. 77:19.

14   Luke 12:42.

15   Lam. 3:22.

16   Apoc. 1:8.

17   Exod. 3:14.

18   Ibid.

19   Ps. 137:6.

20   Compare Ps. 70:12.

21   Compare 1 Pet. 5:6, Luke 14:11, 18:14. Dhuoda shows her indebtedness to Benedictine spirituality in her emphasis on the dialectic of pride and humility. She develops this notion in her third book. The prologue of Benedict's Rule offered exactly this language to describe the dialectic of pride and humility according to which monasticism defined human experience. Dhuoda, in adopting this understanding, blurs the line between secular and religious life.

22   Compare Ps. 102:14.

23   Ps. 52:3.

24   Prudentius, *Cathemerinon* 2:105–8, ed. M. Lavarenne (Paris: Belles Lettres, 1943), 11.

25   Ps. 112:3.

26   The comparison of the day, of human life, and of time was a common patristic

theme, as Riché notes (Dhuoda, 103 n. 4). See, for example, Gregory the Great, *Homilia in evangelia* 1.19, PL 76, 1155.

27 2 Tim. 2:19.

28 Rom. 11:33.

29 Rom. 11:34.

30 Ps. 88:7.

31 2 Par. 6:30.

32 Ps. 96:9.

33 See Riché's comment on this passage (Dhuoda, 104 n. 1). Dhuoda may refer here to Augustine in *Tractatus in Iohannem* 29.4, CC 36, 286, where he remarks on the number of syllables in God's name. She had another source for her discussion of the four letters in the Latin word, perhaps Jerome in *Epistolae* 25, ed. Jérôme Labourt (Paris: 1949–63), 2, 14, or Augustine in *Quaestiones in heptateuchem* 2.120, PL 34, 638.

34 Compare 1 Kings 13:13.

35 With her discussion of God's name and its numerological significance, Dhuoda reveals the fascination with numbers she develops in her ninth book. Her discussion there, as here, is largely based on Isidore of Seville, *Liber numerorum*, PL 83, 179–200. For an introduction to medieval thought on the significance of the numbers one through five, see Vincent H. Hopper, *Medieval Number Symbolism: Its Sources, Meaning, and Influence on Thought and Expression* (New York: Columbia University Press, 1938), esp. 55–58.

36 Here, Dhuoda makes no attempt to associate active life with the role of the lay nobility, or contemplative life with monasticism. She seems to suggest that her son, as a pious layman, will have access to both aspects of Christian conduct.

37 Job 38:7.

38 Job 38:4.

39 Job 38:5.

40 Job 38:8.

41 Job 38:9.

42 Compare Prudentius, *Cathemerinon* 9.13–15, ed. Lavarenne, 50.

43 Ps. 21:29.

44 Compare Dan. 3:100, 4:31.

45 Ps. 23:1.

46 Ps. 8:9.

47 Ps. 94:4.

48   Esther 13:9.

49   Dan. 7:14.

50   Dhuoda means to emphasize her own mortality.

51   Compare Ps. 103:2.

52   Ps. 106:1, 117:1.

53   As Riché notes (Dhuoda, 113 n. 6), Dhuoda's theme here was frequently dis-
      cussed by a variety of Latin Fathers.

54   Ps. 112:4.

55   Acts 17:28.

56   Ps. 103:13.

57   Ps. 144:16.

58   Compare Ps. 5:13.

59   John 14:6.

60   Job 40:2.

61   Job 40:5.

62   See Dhuoda's use of the mirror image in her prologue.

63   Compare Gen. 37:27.

64   Here Dhuoda makes one of her few identifiable references to a saint's life: *Pas-
      sio S. Symphoriani* 11, AASS, Aug. 4, 497. She will refer again to this text in
      Book 7.3, where Dhuoda mentions the saint's mother and her salutary influ-
      ence on him.

BOOK 2

1   As Riché emphasizes (Dhuoda, 118 n. 1), Dhuoda is concerned to educate her
      son against a variety of heresies widespread in southern Frankish dominions
      in the eighth and ninth centuries.

2   Compare 1 Cor. 13:12. Dhuoda, in her remarks about the sublime topic of
      Trinity, here uses the image of the mirror that she employs in her prologue for
      her own small book.

3   Compare Gen. 18:2. As Riché notes (Dhuoda, 119 n. 2), Dhuoda's interpre-
      tation reflects Augustine, *City of God* 16.29; Gregory, *Homilia in evangelia*
      1.18, PL 76, 1152.

4   Riché notes several sources for the Trinitarian interpretation of this scriptural
      text (Dhuoda, 119 n. 3), among them Hilary of Poitiers, *De trinitate* 4.25, PL
      10, 115, and Ambrose, *De fide* 1.13, PL 16, 547.

5   Ps. 66:7–8.

6   Ps. 66:8.

7   Rom. 11:36.

8   Compare Dan. 3:50.

9   Ibid.

10   1 Cor. 13:13.

11   Ps. 141:6.

12   Ps. 36:3–7.

13   Compare Ps. 36:3.

14   As Riché notes, Dhuoda's philological interests here lead her to repeat the etymology of the encyclopedist Isidore (Dhuoda, 124 n. 3): *Origines* 8.2, PL 82, 296.

15   1 John 4:16.

16   Prov. 8:17.

17   Apoc. 3:20.

18   Osee 14:5.

19   John 14:23.

20   Riché here notes the proximity of Dhuoda's prescriptions to a variety of evidence for Benedictine practice (Dhuoda, 125 n. 9), esp. Benedict, Rule 20.

21   Isidore, *Origines* 1.5, PL 82, 81.

22   Compare Benedict, Rule 7.

23   Compare Matt. 7:7–8.

24   Compare Benedict, Rule 7.

25   Compare *Libellus precum*, PL 101, 1401 and 1406. Dhuoda's prayers are similar (see notes below) to texts among a variety of extant Carolingian collections. She seems likely to have selected, for her son's use, her favorites from among such prayer books. Riché (Dhuoda, 127 n. 4) discusses contemporary prayer collections in his introduction to Dhuoda's text (30).

26   Ps. 69:2; compare *Libellus precum*, PL 101, 1404.

27   Ps. 16:8.

28   Compare Gen. 28:12.

29   As Riché notes (Dhuoda, 129 n. 5), Dhuoda's counsel that her son use the sign of the cross is among early evidence for this practice.

30   Compare *Precum libelli quattuor aevi Karolini*, ed. D. A. Wilmart (Rome: Ephemerides Liturgicae, 1940), 55.

31   Dhuoda means the members of her family.

32   Ps. 132:2–3.

33   Dhuoda means if she has grandchildren.

34   Compare Ps. 43:26.

35 Ps. 5:4.

36 Eph. 6:15.

37 Ps. 118:164. Dhuoda here describes as appropriate for a pious layman the observation of quasi-monastic patterns of prayer. Riché notes (Dhuoda, 131 n. 6) the similarity of her advice to that of Carolingian prayer books and even to Alcuin's advice to Charlemagne: see *Precum libelli* 24–25; Alcuin, *Epistolae* 304, MGH Epist. 4, 462.

38 Ps. 16:5.

39 Ps. 85:11.

40 Ps. 85:17.

BOOK 3

1 Ecclus. 3:3. Dhuoda here assumes a traditional attribution of this Old Testament book to David's son.

2 Ecclus. 3:6.

3 Ecclus. 3:7.

4 Ecclus. 3:5.

5 Ecclus. 3:8.

6 Exod. 20:12.

7 Ecclus. 7:30.

8 Compare Ecclus. 3:2.

9 Ecclus. 3:14.

10 Ecclus. 3:15.

11 Dhuoda here clearly alludes to the conflict among Louis the Pious and his sons. As Riché notes (Dhuoda, 136 n. 3), Rabanus Maurus discussed the same family violence a decade earlier. Like Dhuoda, Rabanus saw the analogy of this strife to biblical events: *Liber de reverentia filiorum erga patres et erga reges.* MGH Epist. 5, 403–5.

12 1 Kings 4:11. As Riché notes (Dhuoda, 137 n. 4), violence among the sons of Elias was a common patristic theme. See also Pierre Riché, *Education and Culture in the Barbarian West from the Sixth through the Eighth Century*, trans. John J. Contreni (Columbia: University of South Carolina Press, 1976), 448–49.

13 Dhuoda here perhaps uses a transliterated Greek word, *dyndrum*, for *dendron*; see Riché (Dhuoda, 137 n. 5). Again, Dhuoda is simply ornamenting her Latin with Greek borrowed from an unidentified Latin source.

14 Compare 2 Kings 18:15.

15 Deut. 27:16.

16 Lev. 20:9.

17 Gen. 37:8.

18 Benedict, Rule 34.

19 In recalling Benedict's opening words, Dhuoda affirms what she sees as the proximity of lay and monastic piety. Benedict enjoins in the prologue to his Rule: "Listen carefully, my son, to the master's instructions, and attend to them with the ear of your heart. This is advice from a father who loves you; welcome it, and faithfully put it into practice" (*RB 1980: The Rule of St. Benedict*, ed. Timothy Fry [Collegeville, Minn.: Liturgical Press, 1981], 157). Dhuoda clearly aggrandizes her maternal authority by likening it to abbatial, paternal authority.

20 Prov. 16:21.

21 Prov. 4:10.

22 Ps. 36:9.

23 Ibid.

24 Ps. 26:13.

25 Dhuoda's remarks here about the insignificance of worldly power show some confusion. She generally argues that temporal and spiritual preferment are parallel.

26 1 Pet. 2:13–14.

27 Dhuoda seems to mean specifically that Bernard's position has brought William close to Charles the Bald. As Riché notes (Dhuoda, 141 n. 4), her use of the term *senioratus*, "rank," represents technical feudal language unusual in her text.

28 Compare Gen. 9:26–27.

29 Compare Gen. 9:22. Dhuoda quickly passes over Noah's third son, who saw his father drunken and naked and did not cover him.

30 Gen. 21:6.

31 Gen. 22:17. In fact, Dhuoda quotes God's blessing on Jacob's grandfather Abraham.

32 Gen. 35:10.

33 Gen. 32:28.

34 Compare Jer. 27:12.

35 Gen. 49:22.

36 Compare ibid.

37 Ps. 83:8.

38 As Riché notes (Dhuoda, 147 n. 5), Dhuoda uses the same language for merito-
    rious action in the verse section of her prologue.

39 Compare Luke 2:51.

40 Compare Luke 2:52.

41 William served Charles, later known as "the Bald."

42 Charles's father was, of course, the emperor Louis the Pious, the only one of
    Charlemagne's sons to have survived him, and his mother was Louis's second
    wife, Judith, the daughter of the great Welf ducal house of Bavaria. Charles
    was Louis and Judith's only child. Louis's other sons, Lothar and Louis the
    German, were much older, the products of his first marriage.

    When Dhuoda began her work, Charles was only seventeen but was
    strongly holding his own in his struggle with his half-brothers over their
    father's dominions. When Dhuoda refers to Charles, she therefore describes
    William's relationship to a powerful lord who was little older than William
    and whose experience was markedly close to the biblical family disruption on
    which she dwells in this book.

43 Gen. 24.

44 Compare 3 Kings 2.

45 Rom. 13:1–2.

46 Dhuoda's insistence that no one in William's ancestry had ever betrayed his
    lord seems anxious, especially since Bernard, the boy's father, was clearly
    under suspicion of disloyalty at the time—as he had been for much of his
    career.

47 1 Macc. 3:60.

48 In his introduction to Dhuoda's work, Riché (25) discusses the importance of
    the king's counselors.

49 Ecclus. 32:24.

50 2 Kings 19:29.

51 Dhuoda is here recalling the craftsmanship through which the many magnifi-
    cent books of her period were enriched. It is suggestive of the lay appreciation
    of Carolingian art, as well as of the author herself, that the image of beauty
    she chooses should be manuscript decoration.

52 Compare Ps. 118:103.

53 Compare Prov. 22:1.

54 Compare Cant. 4:11.

55 Ps. 11:7.

56 Compare Ecclus. 6:5.

57 Compare Ps. 50:9.

58 Compare Ps. 62:6.

59 Dhuoda has enjoined her son to "fear, love, and be faithful to" his father. She uses the same terms for her son's adherence to his heavenly Lord.

60 James 1:5–6.

61 Matt. 7:7.

62 Compare Mark 11:24.

63 Wisd. 9:4.

64 Wisd. 9:10.

65 Compare 3 Kings 3:9.

66 Ecclus. 25:5.

67 Compare Ps. 70:17–18.

68 Ibid.

69 Compare Benedict, Rule 63.

70 Dhuoda here adopts the patristic convention of victory in athletic or military competition as an image for salvation.

71 Gen. 41:13ff.

72 Dan. 2:27ff., 5:17, 6:3.

73 Exod. 18:14–23.

74 Jth. 5:5ff.

75 Wisd. 3:5.

76 Wisd. 3:6.

77 1 Macc. 3:60.

78 2 Cor. 11:23. As Riché notes (Dhuoda, 159 n. 8), Dhuoda here refers back to the self-depreciation of her prologue. She is, on the other hand, William's counselor, as he will be the counselor of the great, so she sees her role as important.

79 Dhuoda seems not so much to perceive a decline from a past ideal as to focus on the particular disruption of her own generation.

80 Matt. 24:12.

81 Compare Isidore, *Synonyma* 2.44, PL 83, 355.

82 Jer. 8:22.

83 Compare 1 Kings 22:14.

84 Dhuoda means if William becomes one of the king's counselors, as was his father.

85 Compare Isidore, *Synonyma* 2.43, PL 83, 355.

86 Ibid. 2.37, PL 83, 354.

87 2 Kings 16:15ff.

88 Esther 6:4ff.

89 1 Kings 21:7, 22:9.

90 Esther 8:2ff.

91 Compare 2 Kings 17:14.

92 Ibid.

93 2 Kings 15:32ff.

94 The king David.

95 Esther 6:6ff.

96 Compare Esther 2:22.

97 As Riché notes (Dhuoda, 164 n. 1), Dhuoda may have drawn this speech from some commentary on Esther, a popular topic in ninth-century discussion, since Mardochai's words here are not part of the biblical text.

98 Ps. 7:15–16.

99 Job 12:16.

100 Again and again Dhuoda emphasizes that faithful action yields both heavenly and earthly rewards. See the similar point in her prologue's verse section.

101 Interestingly, here at least Dhuoda does not mention Charles's powerful maternal relations, perhaps because they were outside of the local struggle for hegemony in west Francia, the struggle in which Dhuoda's family was involved.

102 2 Kings 1:25.

103 2 Kings 1:27.

104 2 Kings 1:26.

105 2 Kings 1:23.

106 2 Kings 1:22.

107 Again Dhuoda mentions that she has dictated her handbook to a scribe, but she here affirms that her own choice has governed the contents of her work.

108 2 Kings 1:23.

109 Charles's treatment of Dhuoda's son William—indeed the general pattern of Charles's reign—is as yet unclear at the time of Dhuoda's writing; see Riché's introduction (Dhuoda, 24).

110 Compare Gen. 15:4ff.

111 Clearly God did not see fit to do so in the prior decade, in which Louis the Pious's progeny struggled against their father and each other.

112 As Riché notes (Dhuoda, 169 n. 6), Dhuoda here borrows her language from the litanies of the saints.

113 Compare Gen. 49:22.

114 Ps. 8:3.

115 Compare Phil. 2:7.

116 Compare Luke 14:11, 18:14. This scriptural notion is an important—even central—element in the Benedictine world view. See Benedict, Rule 7.

117 Compare Isa. 60:22.

118 Ps. 148:12.

119 Ps. 150:5.

120 Acts 10:34–35.

121 Dhuoda again refers to the Apostle Paul. Compare Gal. 6:2.

122 Rom. 15:1.

123 2 Cor. 8:14.

124 Gen. 16:12.

125 2 Cor. 9:17.

126 James 1:17.

127 Dhuoda here seems improbably naive, but she is perhaps only restating the Golden Rule (Matt. 7:12) in a fashion compatible with her ensuing grammatical exploration of this theme.

128 What Dhuoda means here is obscure. As Riché notes (Dhuoda, 176–77 nn. 4–6), she seems to be arguing that grammar proves the reciprocity of human actions. Her citations are to a versified version of Donatus's grammar: compare *Ars minor*, ed. Heinrich Keil, *Grammatici Latini* 4 (Leipzig, 1864), 360. Alcuin was also fond of such citations: compare *Grammatica*, PL 101, 875.

129 Dhuoda seems to use Greek window dressing. As Riché notes (Dhuoda, 179 n. 2), her *anefari*, "hold up," is not a Latin word but perhaps derived from the Greek *anaphero*. The original source of Dhuoda's account of the behavior of harts is Pliny's *Natural History* 8.14, although she probably knew it from an intermediary.

130 Acts 4:34.

131 Acts 4:32.

132 Ibid.

133 Compare Luke 1:69.

134 Compare Luke 1:78.

135 Phil. 3:20.

136 Job 12:7–8.

137 As Riché notes (Dhuoda, 182 n. 1), these verses correspond only loosely to a variety of known Carolingian and earlier texts on the same theme.

138 Again, Dhuoda's source is unknown; see Riché (Dhuoda, 183 n. 2). Compare Gen. 2:24.

139 This part, at least, of Dhuoda's poem is drawn from Prudentius; see Riché (Dhuoda, 183 n. 3). Compare Prudentius, *Cathemerinon* 3.36–40, ed. Lavarenne, 13.

140 Here Dhuoda refers to a basic patristic understanding of the place of human history in the cosmic plan. The text from which she is likely to have drawn it is Gregory the Great's *Homilia in evangelia* 34.7, PL 76, 1249. But the idea was not new to Gregory. See especially Augustine, *City of God* 15.1; *Enchiridion* 9.29. Riché (Dhuoda, 33 n. 3) compares these texts with Dhuoda's in his note on the passage where she resumes this discussion in Book 9.4.

141 Compare above.

142 Augustine opens his own autobiographical work with the same scriptural phrase: *Confessions* 1.1. Compare Ps. 144:3.

143 Mark 10:14.

144 Reverence for the clergy, Dhuoda's topic here, was an important theme of Carolingian moral literature, as Riché notes (Dhuoda, 185 n. 4). See especially Jonas of Orléans, *De institutione laicali* 1.20, PL 106, 208.

145 Matt. 26:28.

146 Lev. 11:44.

147 Heb. 12:14.

148 Isa. 61:6.

149 Osee 4:8.

150 Ps. 94:6–7.

151 Compare Ps. 15:8.

152 As Riché notes (Dhuoda, 187 n. 9), Dhuoda here reveals the sort of grammatical and philological education to which she has been exposed.

153 Dhuoda refers to the proem to the mass; see Riché (Dhuoda, 188 n. 1). She also alludes to her preceding discussion (Book 3.10) of how both harts and men hold up their hearts to God.

154 Phil. 3:20.

155 Compare Isidore, *Origines* 7.12, PL 82.

156 Compare Augustine, *City of God* 19.19. As Riché notes (Dhuoda, 188 n. 4), Dhuoda may also have learned this etymology from Rabanus Maurus: *De clericorum institutione* 1.5, PL 107, 301.

157 As Riché notes (Dhuoda, 189 n. 5), Dhuoda may have derived the etymology

of *pontifex* from a text attributed to Alcuin: *Liber de divinis officiis,* PL
101, 1236.

158 Matt. 2:12.

159 Compare Isa. 52:7.

160 Compare Matt. 18:18.

161 Osee 4:8.

162 Jer. 16:16.

163 3 Kings 8:6.

164 Mal. 2:7.

165 Compare Isa. 60:8.

166 Compare Ps. 131:9.

167 Compare 1 Kings 24:5–6.

168 Matt. 7:16.

169 Compare 2 Tim. 2:19.

170 Compare Ps. 32:12.

171 Compare Matt. 11:10.

172 Ps. 104:15.

173 John 14:2.

174 1 Cor. 15:41.

175 Compare Dan. 12:3.

176 3 Kings 8:46.

177 Compare Job 14:5. As Riché notes (Dhuoda, 196 n. 2), Dhuoda seems here to refer to the *Vetus Latina,* a pre-Vulgate version of the Bible text used in patristic
sources.

178 Compare Isidore, *Synonyma* 1.53, PL 83, 839.

179 Compare Ps. 54:24.

180 Compare Heb. 5:6.

BOOK 4

1 Here Dhuoda adverts to the common sense of the classical herbal medical
tradition. The moral application of such knowledge has a lengthy tradition,
as Riché notes (Dhuoda, 198 n. 1): see Cassian, *Institutes* 12.8, CSEL 17, 210;
Gregory the Great, *Moralia in Job* 24.2, PL 76, 287; Isidore, *Sententiae* 2.37,
PL 83, 658; Ambrosius Autpertus, *De conflictu vitiorum et virtutum,* PL 83,
1131–44.

2 Eph. 6:12.

3 Compare Isidore, *Synonyma* 1.7, PL 83, 829.

4   Job 12:6.

5   Job 5:2.

6   Wisd. 2:24.

7   Compare Prudentius, *Cathemerinon* 9.55, ed. Lavarenne, 52; 6.141, ed. Lavarenne, 37.

8   1 Pet. 5.8.

9   Dhuoda refers to the cross.

10 Prudentius, *Cathemerinon* 6.147–48, ed. Lavarenne, 37. Compare 9.52–53, 57, ed. Lavarenne, 51–52.

11 Dhuoda reverts to her consistent theme of corresponding responsibilities in earthly and heavenly spheres.

12 Compare Job 39:13. As Riché notes (Dhuoda, 202 n.1), Dhuoda here borrows from some patristic source based on Pliny's *Natural History* 10.22, if not from Pliny himself.

13 Ecclus. 44:1.

14 Here as elsewhere, especially in the prologue and the conclusion of her work, Dhuoda's depreciation of her status may be more rhetorical than sincere. She certainly believes that her son, at least, has the possibility of becoming a great man on his father's model.

15 Dhuoda seems to confuse scriptural images. Compare Exod. 28:29, 39:14; Apoc. 14:1.

16 Dhuoda mixes imagery from the Old and New Testaments, but not from Ezechiel at all: compare Isa. 6:2–3, Apoc. 4:8.

17 See above for Dhuoda's conflation of images from a variety of scriptural texts.

18 As Riché notes (Dhuoda, 205 n.6), Dhuoda has discussed William's accomplishment of a similarly happy life-path in the verse section of her prologue.

19 William is, of course, a soldier in Charles the Bald's service, but his mother means that he will do battle in a broader sense. Dhuoda consistently uses a martial term, *militari*, to refer to the struggle of secular life. In this usage, she reflects the essential definition of her and her son's social group as a warrior class, as well as reflects the Christian commonplace that Jesus' followers are his earthly army.

20 Gal. 5:16–17.

21 Compare Heb. 11:33.

22 Ps. 70:18.

23 Compare Ps. 77:10.

24 Compare Ps. 102:19.

25   Ps. 83:8.

26   Eph. 5:16.

27   Matt. 24:24.

28   2 Tim. 3:1–4.

29   Ps. 34:1–2.

30   Ps. 139:8.

31   Ps. 31:7.

32   Compare Ps. 34:3, Gen. 26:24.

33   Gen. 15:1.

34   As Riché points out (Dhuoda, 209 n.7), a number of Carolingian moral hand-books discuss the problem of pride: see, for instance, Alcuin, *Liber de virtutibus et vitiis* 23, PL 101, 630; Jonas of Orléans, *De institutione laicali* 3.4, PL 106, 238–41; Paulinus, *Liber exhortationis*, PL 99, 228–29.

35   James 4:6. See Book 3.10, where Dhuoda has raised the theme of pride in terms reflecting Benedictine usage.

36   Matt. 11:29.

37   As Riché notes (Dhuoda, 210 n.2), Dhuoda's description resembles Smaragdus's: *Via regia* 21, PL 102, 960.

38   Riché notes (Dhuoda, 211 n.3) that Dhuoda is here indirectly indebted to patristic sources. Her direct source may have been Jonas of Orléans, *De institutione laicali* 3.4, PL 106, 240, or Smaragdus, *Diadema* 11, PL 102, 603.

39   Isa. 66:2.

40   As Riché explains (Dhuoda, 211 n.5), the theme of the seven gifts of the Holy Spirit was a frequent topic of the Latin Fathers and was occasionally resumed in the Carolingian period, although Dhuoda develops it here with heavy dependence on no known source.

41   Matt. 11:30.

42   Compare *Passio SS. apostolorum Petri et Pauli* 60, ed. R. A. Lipsius, *Acta apostolorum apocrypha* (Leipzig, 1891), 1, 171. Dhuoda here makes one of her few references to a hagiographical text.

43   As Riché notes (Dhuoda, 213 n.3), Augustine's sermon for this occasion is preserved, but his is not the text to which Dhuoda refers.

44   Ps. 73:20.

45   Ps. 73:19.

46   Dhuoda discusses the beatitudes in Book 4.8.

47   Eccles. 11:2.

48   Isa. 11:2–3.

49   As Riché notes (Dhuoda, 214 n. 4), Dhuoda here draws from a definition, originally Gregory the Great's (*Dialogi* 4.3, PL 77, 321), that eventually passed into school books.

50   Dhuoda's Book 10 will explore the sacred importance of numbers. Compare Apoc. 4:5 and Isidore, *Liber numerorum* 8, PL 83, 186.

51   Ecclus. 1.1.

52   Ibid.

53   Compare Wisd. 10:17.

54   Unaccountably, Dhuoda misidentifies this text. Compare Job 36:23.

55   John 8:28.

56   Again, compare Dhuoda's conviction of reward for earthly merits as expressed in her prologue's verse section.

57   Ps. 118:34.

58   Wisd. 1:7.

59   John 3:8.

60   Compare Acts 2:13–15.

61   Mark 16:20.

62   Aggeus 1:1.

63   Apoc. 1:3.

64   1 Cor. 12:8.

65   1 Cor. 12:11.

66   John 4:24.

67   Ps. 50:12.

68   Ps. 50:13.

69   Ps. 50:14.

70   Prov. 4:23.

71   Ps. 33:14.

72   Titus 2:12.

73   Compare Ps. 50:12–14.

74   Since Dhuoda has spoken above of the Spirit's sevenfold—rather than threefold—grace, she may here mean the description of the Spirit she has just offered: "right, holy, and perfect."

75   Compare Apoc. 12:9 and Heb. 11:34. As Riché notes (Dhuoda, 223 n. 2), Dhuoda seems to refer to an unknown source conflating these scriptural images.

76   1 Pet. 5:8–9.

77   Ps. 63:3.

78 As Riché notes (Dhuoda, 223 n. 5), Dhuoda here opposes luxury to chastity, as do other Carolingian authors. Compare Ambrosius Autpertus, *De conflictu vitiorum et virtutum*, PL 83, 1143; Halitgerus Cambrensis, *De paenitentia*, PL 105, 668.

79 Compare Gen. 39:7–20, Dan. 13:45–64.

80 Heb. 13:4.

81 Compare Ps. 72:27.

82 1 Cor. 6:18.

83 Ecclus. 18:30.

84 Ecclus. 18:31.

85 Isa. 51:23.

86 Compare 2 Cor. 12:7.

87 Ps. 73:19.

88 Ecclus. 23:5.

89 Ecclus. 23:10.

90 Job 31:1.

91 Jer. 9:21.

92 Matt. 5:28.

93 Matt. 6:22.

94 Ps. 118:37.

95 Compare Alcuin, *Liber de virtutibus et vitiis* 18, PL 101, 626.

96 Compare Ambrosius Autpertus, *De conflictu vitiorum et virtutum* 79, PL 83, 1143, and Alcuin, *Liber de virtutibus et vitiis* 18, PL 101, 627.

97 As Riché notes (Dhuoda, 228 n. 1), Jonas of Orléans devoted the second book of *De institutione laicali* to married life, drawing on such earlier works as Augustine's *De bono coniugali* and texts of Bede and Isidore.

98 Dhuoda's clear concern here is to establish marriage—and therefore the life of the lay nobility—as a pathway to salvation that is as valid as monastic celibacy. Her own lay status emphasizes her legitimation of marriage stronger than does the sanction of marriage in the texts of the clerical commentators from whom she draws.

99 Prov. 15:15.

100 As Riché notes (Dhuoda, 229 n. 3), Dhuoda here uses the transliterated Greek, *heia*, known to other Carolingian authors.

101 Matt. 5:8.

102 Eccles. 7:10.

103   As Riché notes (Dhuoda, 230 n. 1), Dhuoda's verse source is unidentified. Compare James 1:19.

104   Ps. 30:10.

105   James 1:20.

106   Ps. 4:5.

107   Rom. 12:18.

108   As Riché again notes (Dhuoda, 231 n.7), Dhuoda here copies a poem only loosely similar to any known source.

109   Rom. 12:19, 21.

110   Num. 12:7. This text refers to Moses.

111   Num. 12:3.

112   Compare Exod. 33:11.

113   Exod. 32:14.

114   Exod. 8:10.

115   Compare Deut. 34:7.

116   Luke 14:32.

117   Prov. 16:32.

118   James 1:19.

119   Luke 21:19.

120   Prov. 15:15.

121   Matt. 5:9.

122   Matt. 5:4.

123   1 Par. 29:5; compare Ps. 38:13.

124   Deut. 10:19.

125   Job 31:32.

126   Ps. 67:6; compare Job 29:16.

127   Job 29:16.

128   Ps. 9:17.

129   Ps. 33:7.

130   As Riché notes (Dhuoda, 239 nn.7–8), Dhuoda's precise source is unknown. Compare Gregory, *Moralia in Job* 15.56, 65, PL 75, 1114.

131   Ecclus. 25:3–4.

132   Ps. 39:18.

133   Ps. 21:7.

134   Ps. 119:5.

135   Acts 9:31.

136 Ps. 17:3.

137 Ps. 39:18.

138 Ps. 12:6.

139 Ps. 7:18.

140 Compare Ps. 33:2.

141 Ps. 21:6.

142 Compare Luke 3:16.

143 Ps. 106:28–30.

144 Ps. 135:2–3.

145 Ibid.

146 Compare Apoc. 5:9.

147 Ps. 135:1.

148 Ps. 111:1.

149 Ps. 111:2–3.

150 As Riché notes (Dhuoda, 243 n. 8), Dhuoda may here refer to the Merovingian *Versum de castitate*, MGH, PAC 4, pt. 2, 573.

151 Riché speculates (Dhuoda, 244 n. 1) that Dhuoda here cites an unknown pre-Carolingian source.

152 Compare Ps. 83:8.

153 Matt. 5:8.

154 Matt. 5:3.

155 Ps. 10:8.

156 Wisd. 1:1.

157 Ps. 57:2.

158 Matt. 7:2.

159 Ps. 10:6.

160 Although Riché supposes that Dhuoda's source here may be a collection of monastic anecdotes (Dhuoda, 246 n. 1), it is unidentifiable.

161 Compare Ps. 74:5.

162 As Riché points out (Dhuoda, 246 n. 4), Dhuoda's source is unknown.

163 As Riché notes (Dhuoda, 247 n. 5), Dhuoda's language here reflects the priest's second prayer before the eucharist in the Roman usage.

164 Eph. 5:15.

165 1 Thess. 4:4.

166 Eph. 4:24; compare 1 Thess. 4:4.

167 Ps. 118:112.

168 Isa. 10:1.

134

169   Ps. 36:14.

170   Matt. 24:19.

171   Job 21:13.

172   Compare Mark 8:36.

173   1 John 2:17.

174   Ps. 118:137.

175   Ps. 118:75.

176   Ps. 118:151.

177   Ps. 118:121.

178   Compare Ps. 118:165, 118:147.

179   Compare Jer. 31:12.

180   Matt. 5:6.

181   John 6:27.

182   Ps. 77:25.

183   John 6:35.

184   Compare John 6:27.

185   Compare Ps. 127:3.

186   Compare James 2:13.

187   Luke 6:36.

188   Matt. 5:7.

189   As Riché notes (Dhuoda, 252 n. 1), Dhuoda's use of *condix*—here translated as
       "in his generosity," from its possible derivation from *condere*—is otherwise
       unknown. Her source is likewise unidentified.

190   Matt. 5:4.

191   Ibid.

192   Eph. 5:5.

193   Ps. 40:2.

194   Prov. 28:27.

195   Prov. 3:9.

196   Luke 16:9.

197   Compare Ecclus. 29:15.

198   Luke 6:38.

199   Luke 11:41.

200   Tob. 4:11.

201   Compare Ecclus. 3:33.

202   Luke 6:37.

203   Compare Matt. 5:23.

204 Compare Matt. 5:23–24.

205 2 Tim. 4:2. Here, as in other instances, Dhuoda takes characteristic and scriptural usages of the Rule of St. Benedict and casts them as appropriate to secular life. Compare Benedict, Rule 2.

206 1 Cor. 4:21.

207 Ibid.

208 Compare Ecclus. 4:2.

209 Compare Tob. 4:16.

210 Matt. 7:12.

211 Isa. 58:7.

212 Gen. 2:23.

213 As Riché points out (Dhuoda, 259 n. 2), Dhuoda's etymology—although it effectively serves her rhetorical purpose here—is bogus.

214 Isa. 58:8.

215 Compare Ps. 88:15.

216 Isa. 58:9.

BOOK 5

1 2 Cor. 7:10.

2 As Riché notes (Dhuoda, 261 n. 2), Dhuoda here again uses the metaphor of branching, which she applied to the structure of her entire work at the beginning of her prologue.

3 Compare 2 Cor. 6:10.

4 Dhuoda seems to expand on the explanation of an unknown source, apparently a commentary on Psalm 75, which she directly quotes below. See Riché's remark on this passage (Dhuoda, 262 n. 2).

5 Dhuoda continues her reference to the same source.

6 Compare Eccles. 1:2.

7 Ps. 75:6–7.

8 Compare Isa. 29:8.

9 Ps. 75:6.

10 Job 9:26.

11 Compare Isa. 40:6, in fact not the Psalmist.

12 Job 14:1–2.

13 Job 7:5–6.

14 Compare Ps. 89:4–5.

15 Compare Job 7:1.

16   Job 30:31.

17   Compare Job 29:6.

18   Compare Job 29:7.

19   Compare Job 2:8.

20   Job 21:13.

21   Ps. 75:13.

22   Ecclus. 10:13.

23   Job 14:10.

24   Compare Eccles. 11:3.

25   Eccles. 11:3.

26   Compare Matt. 7:17–20.

27   Matt. 3:10.

28   Compare Gregory, *Moralia in Job* 12.5, PL 75, 990.

29   John 15:5.

30   John 15:16.

31   John 15:5.

32   Compare Ps. 1:3.

33   Compare Jer. 17:8.

34   Eph. 3:17.

35   Gal. 5:22–23.

36   Ps. 24:7.

37   Ps. 27:3.

38   Luke 18:13.

39   Ezech. 33:11.

40   See Book 5.1.

41   1 Cor. 2:9.

42   John 16:22.

43   Ps. 18:13–14.

44   Compare 2 Cor. 12:10.

45   Prov. 4:23.

46   Rom. 5:3.

47   Ps. 119:1.

48   Ps. 80:8.

49   Isa. 49:8.

50   Ps. 117:5.

51   James 1:12.

52   Matt. 5:10–11.

53 Ps. 24:17.

54 Ps. 87:16.

55 Ps. 87:17.

56 Ps. 87:19.

57 Compare Ecclus. 11:27.

58 Prov. 3:11–12.

59 Heb. 12:6.

60 Riché (Dhuoda, 280 n. 3) speculates that Dhuoda here quotes an unknown hagiographical text.

61 Compare 2 Cor. 12:10.

62 Rom. 8:18.

63 Compare Gregory of Tours, *Historia Francorum* 1.24, MGH, SSRM I, 19.

64 Compare Gregory, *Moralia in Job* 2.19, PL 75, 614.

65 Compare Jer. 17:18.

66 Compare John 11:2, Matt. 8:6.

67 John 11:4.

68 Unknown source.

69 Wisd. 3:5.

70 Apoc. 21:4.

71 Compare Gregory, *Moralia in Job* pref. 10, PL 75, 527.

72 Wisd. 3:7.

73 Compare Gregory, *Moralia in Job* pref. 10, PL 75, 528.

74 Compare Ps. 65:10, Ecclus. 2:5.

75 As Riché notes (Dhuoda, 284 n. 1), Dhuoda means to refer to Gregory's *Regula pastoralis* but here has drawn her material (see notes above) from his *Moralia in Job*.

76 Ps. 113:1.

77 Compare 1 Cor. 4:7.

78 Prov. 21:20.

79 Matt. 6:20.

80 As Riché notes (Dhuoda, 285 n. 6), Dhuoda's source here is unknown, but she presumably draws from a saint's life.

81 Matt. 5:3.

BOOK 6

1 As Riché notes (Dhuoda, 286 n. 1), Dhuoda's comparison of the seven gifts and the eight beatitudes was explored by Augustine in *Sermo* 347, PL 39, 1524,

and in *De sermone Domini in monte*, PL 34, 1234. It was then taken up by an anonymous ninth-century author, whose work survives in Laon MS. 75.

2   Compare Heb. 5:12. Although it represents a scriptural reference, Dhuoda's image is an especially appropriate one for a mother writing for her son.

3   Ps. 33:9.

4   Compare 1 Cor. 3:2.

5   Zach. 6:12.

6   Compare 2 Cor. 8:9.

7   Matt. 5:12.

8   Luke 10:20.

9   Dhuoda's meaning is unclear, but Riché's conjecture of *continet* for *conterit* (Dhuoda, 289 n. 6) seems unwarranted. The text might then be translated as "keeps his feet clean of mud and dust" instead of dirtying them.

10   Ps. 14:1.

11   Ps. 14:2–5.

12   Ps. 23:4.

13   Ecclus. 31:10.

14   Compare Ecclus. 7:36.

15   Compare Ps. 14:1.

16   Ecclus. 31:11.

17   Ps. 14:4. As Riché notes (Dhuoda, 291 n. 13), Dhuoda here offers fifteen steps to perfection, analogous to the fifteen steps of the temple in Jerusalem. Compare Isidore, *Liber numerorum* 16.79, PL 83, 194, and Gregory the Great, *Moralia in Job* 35.8, PL 76, 759.

18   Dhuoda here seems to borrow from an unknown contemporary computistical tract. Riché offers bibliographical references for the contemporary computus (Dhuoda, 292 n. 1). His nn. 3–4 suggest sources for some of the numerological lore Dhuoda accumulates here. See also Riché's further notes (Dhuoda, 295 nn. 5–6).

19   Eccles. 11:12.

20   Ps. 50:14.

21   Matt. 18:21.

22   Matt. 18:22.

23   Matt. 6:14.

24   Riché's conjecture of *formantis* for *formantium* (Dhuoda, 294 n. 4) at least makes some sense.

25   As Riché notes (Dhuoda, 295 n. 6), Rabanus Maurus explains otherwise: *Liber*

de computo 6, PL 107, 674. See also E. Alföldi-Rosenbaum, "The Finger-Calculus in Antiquity and in the Middle Ages," *Frühmittelalterliche Studien* 5 (1971): 1–9.

26 Cant. 8:3.

27 4 Kings 20:6.

28 1 Macc. 3:60.

29 Luke 10:20.

BOOK 7

1   Dhuoda's text here is garbled. Riché (Dhuoda, 299 n. 1) suggests an emendation from *contemplatio,* "contemplation," to *contemptio,* "contempt," so that the passage might be translated as "whether you serve as a warrior or have contempt for earthly rank." This change seems discordant with Dhuoda's meaning; she instead raises the—to her—unlikely possibility that her son might become a cleric or a religious. As Riché's note acknowledges, she here presents the traditional opposition of active life and contemplative life.

2   As Riché notes (Dhuoda, 299 n. 3), Dhuoda's identification of this saying with Paul is a misattribution.

3   John 3:3.

4   John 3:6.

5   Ibid.

6   Gal. 4:19.

7   1 Cor. 4:15.

8   See *Passio SS. Iuliani, Basilissae et sociorum,* AASS, Jan. 1, 575–87. As Riché notes (Dhuoda, 300 n. 7), this text enjoyed a wide readership in the Carolingian period.

9   See *Passio S. Symphoriani,* AASS, Aug. 4, 496–97. As Riché again notes (Dhuoda, 301 n. 8), Dhuoda here borrows from a saint's life widely read in her period. Symphorian's mother, whose name is not revealed, called encouragement to her son from the town wall as he was martyred outside Autun. Dhuoda cited the mother's words in Book 1.7.

10 Dhuoda's intent to approximate her teaching of her child to the practices of these holy ladies is clear.

11 As Riché notes (Dhuoda, 302 n. 1), Dhuoda may in this passage be indebted to Paschasius Radbertus, *In Mattheum* 8.16, PL 120, 576.

12 Ps. 88:49.

13 Compare Gen. 6:13, Jer. 22:10.

14   Josue 23:14; compare 3 Kings 18:24.

15   Apoc. 2:11.

16   Apoc. 3:12. Dhuoda here seems to read the voice of the apostle John in his revelation as God's own.

17   Aggeus 2:24.

18   Apoc. 2:7.

19   Compare Alcuin, *Liber de virtutibus et vitiis* 5, PL 101, 616.

BOOK 8

1   1 Thess. 5:17.

2   Compare Lam. 2:18.

3   As Riché notes (Dhuoda, 307 n. 3), this expression is found in several Carolingian prayers: *Precum libelli* 27, 53, 76.

4   Riché here notes (Dhuoda, 307 n. 4) that Dhuoda's prescriptions follow the liturgy for Good Friday. See Josef A. Jungmann, *Missarum sollemnia: Eine genetische Erklärung der römischen Messe*, 4th ed. (Freiburg: Herder, 1958), 2, 271–81.

5   Charles the Bald.

6   Dhuoda seems dubious, not surprising given Bernard's difficulties at and prior to the time of her writing.

7   Phil. 4:7.

8   As Riché notes (Dhuoda, 311 n. 3), Dhuoda here again seems to borrow from a contemporary prayer: see *Precum libelli* 52.

9   See Jungmann, 271–81.

10   As Riché points out (Dhuoda, 312 n. 1), Dhuoda's following discussion of prayers for the dead derives eventually from Augustine, *Enchiridion* 110, but she may know it from Jonas of Orléans's *De institutione laicali* 15, PL 106, 265.

11   Augustine had said, as Riché points out (Dhuoda, 313 n. 3), "for those who were not truly evil."

12   Riché suggests (Dhuoda, 314 n. 1) that Dhuoda here too bases her argument on Augustine's *Enchiridion.*

13   Riché's conjecture of *deviant*, "they stray," for *derivant* "they derive," is likely correct (Dhuoda, 315 n. 2). Dhuoda is here concerned to warn against the anti-Trinitarian heresies that she has mentioned in Book 2.1.

14   Compare Ps. 102:14.

15   2 Cor. 12:21.

16   Rom. 2:12.

17   Matt. 20:7.

18   As Riché notes (Dhuoda, 316 n. 2), Dhuoda's anecdote is based on a passage
      from the *Verba seniorum*, PL 73, 1013. The abbot Macarius is here conversing
      with a pagan priest.

19   Ps. 85:13.

20   Luke 16:27.

21   Matt. 22:13.

22   1 Cor. 10:12.

23   Eph. 5:14.

24   Dhuoda's discussion of prayer suggests that she sees close, as well as more
      distant, relations as integral to her son's lineage.

25   Dhuoda refers William to Book 10.5.

26   Compare Ecclus. 14:4.

27   Dhuoda here makes clear, as Riché notes (Dhuoda, 321 n. 4), that at least some
      of Bernard's territorial possessions may be expected to come to his son.

28   Bernard, the young William's father.

29   Dhuoda clearly draws these prayers from contemporary convention, although
      Riché cites no specific source.

30   2 Macc. 12:46.

31   Tob. 4:20.

BOOK 9

1   Dhuoda here sheds light on her method of composition. Her sources are vari-
     ous, but she has so substantially reworked them that they are difficult to iden-
     tify specifically.

2   As Dhuoda mentioned in Book 6.3, she envisions fifteen steps to perfection
     through the seven gifts of the Holy Spirit and the eight beatitudes. Here she
     seems to be saying in a roundabout way that William's understanding will be
     transformed as he matures.

3   As Riché notes (Dhuoda, 327 n. 5), Dhuoda here draws on Augustine, *Tracta-
     tus in Iohannem* 9.15, CC 36, 98, and 10.12, CC 36, 108, although she perhaps
     knows his discussion from a ninth-century recapitulation.

4   As Riché notes (Dhuoda, 328 n. 1), Dhuoda here seems closely to follow Raba-
     nus Maurus's discussion in *De laudibus S. Crucis* 1.12, PL 107, 198. She has
     used *moida* for the Greek letter on a prior occasion, in the verse section of her
     prologue.

142

5 John 2:19.

6 John 2:21.

7 Ibid.

8 John 19:5.

9 Osee 6:3.

10 Ps. 82:19.

11 Dhuoda refers to the canon tables of the Gospels, through which parallel texts were identified and which were frequently represented in manuscript Bibles as columns bearing the earth.

12 Compare Matt. 25:2.

13 Dhuoda refers to the miracle at the wedding feast of Cana: John 2:6. As Riché points out (Dhuoda, 331 n. 4), Augustine interpreted the urns of water that became wine as a figure for time: *Tractatus in Iohannem* 9.6, CC 36, 94. Compare Isidore, *Origines* 5.38, PL 82, 223, and Rabanus Maurus, *Liber de computo* 96, PL 107, 726.

14 Compare Prudentius, *Cathemerinon* 9.28, ed. Lavarenne, 50.

15 Compare Apoc. 4:5. See also Isidore, *Liber numerorum* 8, PL 83, 186. Dhuoda has used this image in Book 4.4.

16 Gen. 6:18. Compare Isidore, *Liber numerorum* 9, PL 83, 189.

17 As Riché notes (Dhuoda, 332 n. 1), Dhuoda means the orders of the angels. Compare Rabanus Maurus, *De laudibus S. Crucis*, PL 107, 202. Gregory the Great discussed the angel ranks in *Homilia in evangelia* 34.7, PL 76, 1249–50.

18 As Riché notes (Dhuoda, 332 n. 2), Dhuoda develops this discussion in Book 9.4.

19 Compare again Gregory the Great, *Homilia in evangelia* 34.6, PL 76, 1249. As Riché notes (Dhuoda, 333 n. 3), Augustine's development of this notion is basic: *City of God* 22.1; *Enchiridion* 9.29.

20 Rom. 11:25–26.

21 Compare Rabanus Maurus, *De laudibus S. Crucis*, PL 107, 205, who argues instead, as Riché notes (Dhuoda, 333 n. 6), that one thousand signifies perfection.

22 Gen. 24:60. See Riché's note (Dhuoda, 334 n. 1), indicating that Dhuoda meant "thousands of thousands" rather than the simple "thousands," *millia*, offered in the manuscripts.

23 Compare Gen. 28:3.

24 Compare Gen. 27:28.

25 As Riché acknowledges (Dhuoda, 335 n. 4), Dhuoda's reference is unclear.

26 Deut. 28:3.

27 Deut. 28:6.

28 Ps. 70:18.

BOOK 10

1 The first letters of the following stanzas, another acrostic, spell VERSI AD VVILHELMUM F[ILIUM], or "verses to William, my son." These verses form a synopsis of the preceding text. As Riché notes (Dhuoda, 341 n. 4), the form of these stanzas approximates sapphic verse.

2 In Book 1.7, Dhuoda used the same language to describe the composition of and the intended audience for her work.

3 Compare Heb. 4:12.

4 Compare Mark 12:33.

5 As Riché notes (Dhuoda, 343 n. 5), Dhuoda means to refer to Charles the Bald. Although her language is vague, it is similar to her description of the Carolingian house in Book 3.4.

6 Compare Apoc. 2:28.

7 As Riché notes (Dhuoda, 345 n.7), William turned sixteen on November 29, 842.

8 Dhuoda closes her work as she opened it, repeatedly. Her doing so suggests that she set it aside, then took it up again on later occasions.

9 2 Kings 23:8.

10 Rom. 9:16.

11 I Macc. 3:60.

12 John 20:26.

13 Dhuoda may mean William's deceased ancestors, for whom he should pray: see Book 8.14–15. Riché suggests (Dhuoda, 349 n.6) that she means only the great men of the past: see Book 4.1.

14 2 Cor. 11:26.

15 Compare Gen. 7:2.

16 Dhuoda means her support for Bernard's position as count of the Spanish March. As Riché points out (Dhuoda, 353 n.1), Dhuoda uses the feudal term *servitium* for her service to Bernard.

17 As Riché notes (Dhuoda, 353 n. 4), Dhuoda here gives the first extant testimony of the activity of Jews as moneylenders in the south of France.

144

18   The names here have been the subject of much scholarship. They seem to refer to members of Bernard's family, not Dhuoda's, and thus contribute to the mother's emphasis on William's obligation to his patrilineage. Dhuoda surely does not wish her son to ignore his spiritual duty toward the other side of his family, however, for she argues that prayer on her behalf is among his primary responsibilities. See Riché's notes (Dhuoda, 355 nn. 2–11). For a close discussion of who these individuals were, see Bouchard, "Family Structure," esp. 642, 656, and n. 62.

19   Ps. 113:18.

20   As Riché points out (Dhuoda, 356 n. 1), other Carolingian authors, such as Alcuin and Hincmar, likewise composed their own epitaphs.

21   Dhuoda here offers another acrostic. The initial letters of the following verses spell DHUODANE, perhaps an alternate Latin spelling of her name or an adjective form.

22   As Riché notes (Dhuoda, 357 n. 3), Dhuoda abbreviates *dis manibus*, "into the hands of God."

23   Dhuoda uses the Greek letters alpha and omega to invoke Christ. Compare Apoc. 1:8.

BOOK II

1   Much of this book is copied verbatim from Alcuin, *De psalmorum usu liber*, PL 101, 465–68. As Riché notes (Dhuoda, 360 n. 1), Dhuoda's rendering is so faulty as sometimes to obscure Alcuin's meaning. Here, as in the Riché edition's French translation, the sense has occasionally been restored according to Alcuin's text. Riché's notes to this book detail Dhuoda's departures from Alcuin's model (Dhuoda, 360–69).

2   Ps. 49:23.

3   Ps. 6:2, 37:1, 129:2, 142:1, 31:1, 50:3, 129:1.

4   Ps. 16:1, 24:1, 53:3, 66:2, 69:2, 30:2, 85:1.

5   Ps. 140:1, 146:1, 148:1, 102:1 or 103:1.

6   Ps. 21:2, 60:2, 63:2, 11:2.

7   Ps. 41:2, 83:2, 62:2.

8   Ps. 12:1, 43:2, 55:2 or 56:2, 54:2, 30:2.

9   Ps. 33:2, 102:1, 144:1.

10   See Dan. 3:52–90.

11   Ps. 118:1.

12   Dhuoda's heavy dependence on Alcuin ends here.

13   As Riché notes (Dhuoda, 369 n. 2), Dhuoda here quotes the Athanasian creed, which she mentions as well in Book 2.1.

14   November 30, 841.

15   February 2, apparently of 843.

16   Dhuoda anxiously waits for a clear conclusion to the conflict over the succession to Louis the Pious.

17   John 19:30.

Bibliography

EDITIONS AND TRANSLATIONS OF PRIMARY WORKS

Dhuoda. *L'éducation carolingienne: Le Manuel de Dhuoda (843)*. Ed. Edouard Bondurand. Paris, 1887.

Dhuoda. "The Frankish Mother Dhuoda." Trans. James Marchand. In *Medieval Women Writers*, ed. Katharina M. Wilson, 1–29. Athens: University of Georgia Press, 1984.

Dhuoda. "The *Liber Manualis* of Dhuoda: Advice of a Ninth-Century Mother for Her Sons." Ed. and trans. Myra Ellen Bowers. Ph.D. diss., Catholic University, 1977.

Dhuoda. *Manuel pour mon fils*. Ed. Pierre Riché. Trans. Bernard de Vrégille and Claude Mondésert. Sources chrétiennes 225. Paris: Editions du Cerf, 1975.

Godman, Peter, ed. *Poetry of the Carolingian Renaissance*. Norman: University of Oklahoma Press, 1985.

Grat, Félix, et al., eds. *Annales de Saint-Bertin*. Paris: C. Klincksieck, 1964.

Nithard. *Historiarum libri III*. 3d ed., ed. Ernest Müller. MGH SSRG.

Scholz, Bernhard Walter, trans. *Carolingian Chronicles: Royal Frankish Annals and Nithard's Histories*. Ann Arbor: University of Michigan Press, 1970.

Vita de sancto Willelmo duce postea monacho Gellonensi in Gallia. AASS, May 6, 809–22.

Waitz, Georg, ed. *Vita Hludowici imperatoris*. MGH SS 2, 607–48.

DICTIONARIES

DuCange, Charles Dufresne. *Glossarium mediae et infimae latinitatis*. 7 vols. Ed. G.A.L. Henschel. Paris, 1840–50.

Fuchs, J. W., et al., eds. *Lexicon latinitatis nederlandicae medii aevi: Woordenboek van het middeleeuws Latijn van den noordelijke nederlanden.* Vols. 1–. Leiden: E. J. Brill, 1977–.

Latham, R. E. *Revised Medieval Latin Word-List from British and Irish Sources.* London: Oxford University Press, 1965.

Lewis, Charlton T., and Charles Short. *A Latin Dictionary.* Oxford, 1879.

Niermeyer, J. F. *Mediae latinitatis lexicon minus.* Leiden: Brill, 1976.

Prinz, Otto, ed. *Mittellateinisches Worterbuch bis zum ausgehenden 13. Jahrhundert.* Vols. 1–. Munich: Beck, 1967–.

Souter, Alexander. *A Glossary of Later Latin to 600 A.D.* Oxford: Clarendon Press, 1949.

Thesaurus linguae latinae. Vols. 1–. Leipzig: Teubner, 1900–.

SECONDARY WORKS

Alföldi-Rosenbaum, E. "The Finger-Calculus in Antiquity and in the Middle Ages." *Frühmittelalterliche Studien* 5 (1971): 1–9.

Antony, Heinz. "Edition und Lexicographie: Zur Zuverlässigkeit kritischer Apparate." *Deutsches Archiv für Erforschung des Mittelalters* 37 (1981): 774–85.

———. *Fürstenspiegel und Herrscherethos in der Karolinger Zeit.* Bonn: L. Rohrscheid, 1968.

———. "Korruptel oder Lemma? Die Problemmatik der Lexicographie auf dem Hintergrund der Editionen." *Mittellateinisches Jahrbuch* 16 (1981): 288–333.

Bessmertny, Y. "Le monde vu par une femme noble au IXe siècle: La perception du monde dans l'aristocratie carolingienne." *Moyen Age* 93 (1987): 162–84.

Beumann, Helmut. "Topos und Gedankengefüge bei Einhard." *Archiv für Kulturgeschichte* 33 (1951): 337–50.

Bishop, Jane. "Bishops as Marital Advisors." In *Women of the Medieval World: Essays in Honor of John H. Mundy,* ed. Julius Kirschner and Suzanne F. Wemple, 53–84. Oxford: Blackwell, 1985.

Bouchard, Constance B. "Family Structure and Family Consciousness among the Aristocracy in the Ninth to Eleventh Centuries." *Francia* 16 (1986): 639–58.

———. "The Origins of the French Nobility: A Reassessment." *American Historical Review* 86 (1981): 501–32.

Bradley, Ritamary. "Backgrounds of the Title *Speculum* in Medieval Literature." *Speculum* 29 (1954): 100–115.

Contreni, John J. "Carolingian Biblical Studies." In *Carolingian Essays: Andrew W. Mellon Lectures in Early Christian Studies,* ed. Uta-Renate Blumenthal, 71–98. Washington: Catholic University of America Press, 1983.

Bibliography

Dronke, Peter. *Women Writers of the Middle Ages: A Critical Study of Texts from Perpetua (†203) to Marguerite Porete (†1310)*. Cambridge: Cambridge University Press, 1984.

Duby, Georges. *Medieval Marriage: Two Models from Twelfth-Century France*. Baltimore: Johns Hopkins University Press, 1978.

Duckett, Eleanor Shipley. *Alcuin, Friend of Charlemagne: His World and His Work*. Hamden, Conn.: Archon Books, 1951.

———. *Carolingian Portraits: A Study in the Ninth Century*. Ann Arbor: University of Michigan Press, 1962.

Dyer, Joseph. "The Singing of Psalms in the Early-Medieval Office." *Speculum* 64 (1989): 535–78.

Fichtenau, Heinrich. *The Carolingian Empire*. Trans. Peter Munz. Oxford: Blackwell, 1957.

Freed, John B. "Reflections on the Medieval German Nobility." *American Historical Review* 91 (1986): 553–75.

Ganshof, F. L. *The Carolingians and the Frankish Monarchy: Studies in Carolingian History*. Trans. Janet Sondheimer. Ithaca, N.Y.: Cornell University Press, 1971.

———. *Feudalism*. Trans. Philip Grierson. London: Harper and Row, 1961.

Gibson, Margaret, and Janet Nelson, eds. *Charles the Bald: Court and Kingdom*. British Archaeological Reports 101. London: B.A.R., 1981.

Godman, Peter. *Poets and Emperors: Frankish Politics and Carolingian Poetry*. Oxford: Clarendon Press, 1987.

Hannig, Jürgen. *Consensus fidelium*. Stuttgart: A. Hiersemann, 1982.

Hennebicque, Regine. "Structures familiales et politiques au IXe siècle." *Revue historique* 265 (1981): 289–90.

Herlihy, David. "Land, Family, and Women in Continental Europe, 701–1200." *Traditio* 18 (1962): 89–120.

———. *The Social History of Italy and Western Europe, 700–1500: Collected Studies*. London: Variorum Reprints, 1978.

Hopper, Vincent H. *Medieval Number Symbolism: Its Sources, Meaning, and Influence on Thought and Expression*. New York: Columbia University Press, 1938.

Laistner, M.L.W. *Thought and Letters in Western Europe: A.D. 500 to 900*. Ithaca, N.Y.: Cornell University Press, 1957.

Lehmann, Paul. *Mittelalterliche Büchertitel*. 2 vols. Sitzungsberichte der bayerischen Akademie der Wissenschaften, philosophisch-historische Klasse 1948, 1953. Munich: Bayerische Akademie der Wissenschaften, 1949, 1953.

Löfstedt, Bengt. "Zu Dhuodas Liber Manualis." *Arctos* 15 (1981): 67–83.

Lynch, Joseph H. *Godparents and Kinship in Early Medieval Europe.* Princeton: Princeton University Press, 1986.

McKitterick, Rosamond. *The Carolingians and the Written Word.* Cambridge: Cambridge University Press, 1989.

——. *The Frankish Kingdoms under the Carolingians, 751–987.* London: Longman, 1983.

McNamara, JoAnn, and Suzanne F. Wemple. "Sanctity and Power: The Dual Pursuit of Medieval Women." In *Becoming Visible: Women in European History,* ed. Renate Bridenthal and Claudia Koonz, 90–118. Boston: Houghton Mifflin, 1977.

Martindale, Jane. "The French Aristocracy in the Middle Ages: A Reappraisal." *Past and Present* 75 (1977): 5–45.

Misch, Georg. *Geschichte der Autobiographie.* 4 vols. Frankfurt: G. Schulte-Bulmke, 1949–69.

Mohrmann, Christine. *Latin vulgaire, latin des chrétiens, latin médiéval.* Paris: C. Klincksieck, 1955.

Murray, Alexander Callander. *Germanic Kinship Structures.* Toronto: Pontifical Institute of Mediaeval Studies, 1983.

Nelson, Janet L. "Les femmes et l'évangelisation au IXe siècle." *Revue du nord* 68 (1986): 471–85.

——. "On the Limits of the Carolingian Renaissance." In *Renaissance and Renewal in Christian History,* 51–69. Studies in Church History 14, ed. Derek Baker. Oxford: B. Blackwell, 1977.

——. "Public *Histories* and Private History in the Work of Nithard." *Speculum* 60 (1985): 251–93.

Norberg, Dag. *Introduction à l'étude de la versification latine médiévale.* Stockholm: Almqvist and Wiksell, 1958.

——. *La poésie latine rhythmique du haut moyen âge.* Stockholm: Almqvist and Wiksell, 1954.

Poulin, Jean-Claude. *L'idéal de sainteté dans l'Aquitaine carolingienne d'après les sources hagiographiques (750–950).* Travaux du laboratoire d'histoire religieuse de l'Université Laval 1. Quebec: Université Laval, 1975.

Raby, F.J.E. *Christian Latin Poetry from the Beginnings to the Close of the Middle Ages.* Oxford: Clarendon, 1966.

——. *A History of Secular Latin Poetry in the Middle Ages.* 2d ed. 2 vols. Oxford: Clarendon, 1957.

Rand, E. K. "A Vade Mecum of Liberal Culture in a Manuscript of Fleury." *Philological Quarterly* 1 (1922): 258–77.

Repertorium fontium historiae medii aevi, vols. 1–. Rome: Instituto storico italiano per il Medio Evo, 1962–.

Riché, Pierre. "Les bibliothèques de trois aristocrates laics carolingiens." *Moyen Age* 69 (1963): 87–104.

———. *Les écoles et l'enseignement dans l'occident chrétien de la fin du Ve siècle au milieu du IXe siècle.* Paris: Aubier Montaigne, 1979.

———. *Education and Culture in the Barbarian West from the Sixth through the Eighth Century.* Trans. John J. Contreni. Columbia: University of South Carolina Press, 1976.

Rosenwein, Barbara H. *Rhinoceros Bound: Cluny in the Tenth Century.* Philadelphia: University of Pennsylvania Press, 1982.

Schmid, Karl. "The Structure of the Nobility in the Earlier Middle Ages." In *The Medieval Nobility: Studies on the Ruling Classes of France and Germany from the Sixth to the Twelfth Century,* ed. and trans. Timothy Reuter, 39–49. Europe in the Middle Ages: Selected Studies 14. Amsterdam: North Holland Publishing, 1978.

Smalley, Beryl. *The Study of the Bible in the Middle Ages.* Notre Dame, Ind.: University of Notre Dame Press, 1964.

Sot, Michel. "Spiritualité et sainteté chez les grands laics carolingiens. A propos de deux ouvrages récents." *Revue d'histoire de la spiritualité* 52 (1976): 295–301.

Sullivan, Richard E. "The Carolingian Age: Reflections on Its Place in the History of the Middle Ages." *Speculum* 64 (1989): 267–306.

Van Acker, Lieven. "Quelques suggestions à propos du texte du *Liber manualis* de Dhuoda." In *Hommages à Jozef Vermans,* ed. Freddy Decreus and Carl Deroux, 319–27. Collection Latomus 193. Brussels: Latomus, 1986.

Vernet, André. "Un nouveau manuscrit du 'Manuel' de Dhuoda (Barcelone, Biblioteca Central 569)." *Bibliothèque de l'école des chartes* 114 (1956): 20–44.

Wagner, David L., ed. *Seven Liberal Arts in the Middle Ages.* Bloomington: Indiana University Press, 1983.

Wallace-Hadrill, J. M. *The Barbarian West, 400–1000.* London: Hutchinson's University Press, 1952.

———. *The Frankish Church.* Oxford: Oxford University Press, 1983.

Wattenbach-Levison. *Deutschlands Geschichtsquellen im Mittelalter: Vorzeit und Karolinger.* Fasc. 4. Ed. Heinz Lowe. Weimar: Böhlaus Nachfolger, 1957.

Bibliography

Wemple, Suzanne Fonay. *Women in Frankish Society: Marriage and the Cloister,
500–900*. Philadelphia: University of Pennsylvania Press, 1985.

Wollasch, Joachim. "Eine adlige Familie des frühen Mittelalters: Ihr Selbstverständ-
nis und ihre Wirklichkeit." *Archiv für Kirchengeschichte* 39 (1957): 150–88.

Wright, Roger. *Late Latin and Early Romance in Spain and Carolingian France*.
ARCA Classical and Medieval Texts, Papers, and Monographs 8. Liverpool:
F. Cairns, 1982.

Other volumes in the Regents Studies in Medieval Culture include:

Speaking of the Middle Ages
By Paul Zumthor
Translated by Sarah White

Mervelous Signals
Poetics and Sign Theory in the Middle Ages
By Eugene Vance

Giants in Those Days
Folklore, Ancient History, and Nationalism
By Walter E. Stephens

Vilain and Courtois
*Transgressive Parody in French Literature of
the 12th and 13th Centuries*
By Kathryn Gravdal

De Vulgari Eloquentia: *Dante's Book of Exile*
By Marianne Shapiro

Literacy and Power in Anglo-Saxon Literature
By Seth Lerer